THE BASKETBALL QUIZBOOK

THE BASKETBALL QUIZBOOK

Norman MacLean & Norb Ecksl

DRAKE PUBLISHERS INC.
NEW YORK

Published in 1976 by
Drake Publishers Inc.
801 Second Avenue
New York, N.Y. 10017

All rights reserved
© Copyright in 1976 by Norman MacLean

Library of Congress Cataloging in Publication Data

MacLean, Norman.
    The basketball quizbook.

    1. Basketball -- History -- Miscellanea. I. Title.
GV883.M32   796.32'3'09   76-16971
ISBN 0-8473-1323-9 pbk.

Printed in the United States of America

For Jeff who shoots baskets

in his backyard

every day and dreams

of the National Basketball Association.

CONTENTS

Chapter 1
PRO BASKETBALL'S EARLY DAYS
Questions 1   Answers 2
Photo Section 3

Chapter 2
NATIONAL BASKETBALL LEAGUE
Questions 9   Answers 12

Chapter 3
OTHER LEAGUES
Questions 15   Answers 16
Photo Section 18

Chapter 4
AMERICAN BASKETBALL LEAGUE
Questions 21   Answers 22

Chapter 5
NATIONAL BASKETBALL ASSOCIATION (PLAYERS)
Questions 25   Answers 29
Photo Section 34

Chapter 6
AMERICAN BASKETBALL ASSOCIATION
Questions 73   Answers 75
Photo Section 78

Chapter 7
TEAM AND LEAGUE
NATIONAL BASKETBALL ASSOCIATION
Questions 93   Answers 96
Photo Section 100

Chapter 8
GENERAL INFORMATION
Questions 105   Answers 107

Chapter 9
GLOSSARY OF BASKETBALL SLANG 109

PHOTO SECTIONS

Chapter 1
PRO BASKETBALL'S EARLY DAYS

page 3   The Buffalo Germans as Champions in 1901
        4   The Present-day Celtics were Preceded by some Great Players
        5   Nat Holman with the Celtics in 1926
        6   Johnny Beckman / Basketball Hall of Fame 1974
        7   One of the Original Celtics, Joe Lapchick

Chapter 3
OTHER LEAGUES

page 18   Marques Haynes in 1951
       19   Goose Tatum

Chapter 5
NATIONAL BASKETBALL ASSOCIATION (PLAYERS)

page 34   Bob Davies, super star of the Rochester Royals
       35   Clyde Lovelette, Minneapolis Lakers, 1953
       36   Knick Vince Boryla with Vern Mikkelson of Lakers
       37   Andy Phillip of the Chicago Stags
       38   Paul Arizin and Jumping Joe Fulks
       39   Vern Mikkelson of Lakers takes shot against St. Louis
       40   Easy Ed Macauley, part of the starry trio of Bob Cousy, Bill Sharman and Macauley, when he played with Boston
       41   Bob Petit, a super star with the St. Louis Hawks
       42   Dolph Schayes, an NBA star, originally played with the NBL Syracuse Nationals
       43   Maurice Stokes of the Cincinnati Royals with teammate, Jack Twyman
       44   Knicks' Tom Gola
       45   1962 record setting Celtics, with coach Auerbach

46	Royals Oscar Robertson never won a title until he teamed up with Lew Alcindor at Milwaukee
47	1964 Playoff action between San Francisco and Boston
48	A smiling Wilt the Stilt Chamberlain
49	Bob Cousy
50	Elgin Baylor, the man with 1,000 moves
51	Sam Jones when he was the Celtics top back court man
52	The Boston Celtics John Havlicek
53	Detroit's Terry Dischinger
54	Dave Bing
55	Jerry Lucas
56	Bill Bradley, star of two world champion New York Knickerbocker teams in 1970 and 1973
57	Bullets Wes Unseld stopping Willis Reed of the Knicks during 1969 Playoffs
58	Rick Barry of the San Francisco Warriors
59	Jerry West may have had the best outside touch
60	Earl Monroe started with the Baltimore Bullets
61	Bill Russell
62	Gail Goodrich
63	The Big "E" Elvin Hayes
64	Champions Dave DeBusschere, Willis Reed and Bill Bradley of the Knicks
65	Walt "Clyde" Frazier took Bob Cousy's place as the trickiest back court man
66	"The Pistol" Pete Maravich, a big gunner with both the Atlanta Hawks and New Orleans Jazz
67	Jerry West tries to maneuver around Phoenix' Connie Hawkins
68	Milwaukee's Kareem Abdul Jabbar against Lakers' Wilt Chamberlain in 1972 Playoff
69	Wes Unseld of the Bullets outrebounds Dave Cowens of the Celtics
70	K. C. Jones, when he coached the Washington Bullets
71	Lew Alcindor became Kareem Abdul Jabbar

Photo Sections xi

Chapter 6
AMERICAN BASKETBALL ASSOCIATION

- page 78   Alex Hannum, a former coach with Syracuse in the NBA
- 79   Rick Barry made the New York Nets
- 80   Spencer Haywood with the Denver Rockets
- 81   The 1968-69 All League ABA team
- 82   George McGinnis with the Indiana Pacers against Carolina's Billy Cunningham
- 83   The last ABA Commissioner, Dave DeBusschere
- 84   Mike Storen, the fourth Commissioner of the ABA
- 85   George Mikan, the former NBA hero, was the first Commissioner of the ABA
- 86   Wilt the Stilt Chamberlain
- 87   George McGinnis of Indiana outrebounding the Nets Rick Barry and Billy Paultz in 1972
- 88   New York's Julius Erving trying to stop Jumping Joe Caldwell of Carolina
- 89   Artis Gilmore was the best big man developed by the ABA
- 90   Dan Issel, an ABA Dave DeBusschere
- 91   Lou Dampier, the all time champion of the home run, the 3 point ABA bomb

Chapter 7
TEAM AND LEAGUE
NATIONAL BASKETBALL ASSOCIATION

- page 100   Vince Boryla
- 101   Red Auerbach
- 102   Former NBA Commissioner Walter Kennedy
- 103   The Referee's Dean, Mendy Rudolph

FOREWORD

The emergence of basketball from its early days as a side show at the Saturday night dance ended an era which is almost purely fictionalized by most writers. Still, the legend of the Original Celtics, Buffalo Germans, Cleveland Rosenblooms and other early teams is almost magical in comparison to the highly organized National Basketball Association, or even present day collegiate competition.

The American Basketball Association which merged with the NBA is a later day throwback to those early teams. Checks bounced and teams folded, just as they did in the American Basketball League, Eastern Basketball League and countless other pro circuits which failed before the advent of the NBA. And the ABA possessed one player -- Doctor J., Julius Erving, who is rated the best in the game. Who's better, Erving or Dave Cowens is the argument today.

Just after the close of World War II, the Basketball Association of America was formed as a rival to the National Basketball League. The BAA, operating in the larger arenas of the East, had the markets; the Nationals had the players, with giants such as George Mikan dominating the sport. Result -- a merger -- and Mikan and the Minneapolis Lakers became dominant, although always challenged by the Rochester Royals, and a merger which formed the NBA.

Those Royals and the Syracuse Nationals, owned by Dan Biasone, were a throwback to the early dance hall days. Biasone operated a bowling alley, cocktail lounge and dance hall in Syracuse, but it was he who spawned the idea of the 24 second rule which saved the pros.

With the merger of the ABA and NBA, pro basketball encompasses almost every large city in the United States. Its Hot Stove League operates through twelve months of the year. Norman MacLean's *Basketball Quiz Book* is a much asked for work. Trivia experts will delight in the section on the early pros, the "other leagues" and finally the National League. Who were the Fort Wayne Zollner Pistons? They were the forerunners of the Detroit Pistons.

And how about the Tri City Black Hawks? Today they are the Atlanta Hawks, having somehow maintained part of their nicknames through stops in Milwaukee and St. Louis.

There is a special tingle of electricity about being in a basketball arena. Basketball is a special game developed as a winter-time fill-in. Today its scope is world-wide, but it's still a special bit of Americana. When you read *The Basketball Quiz Book* you are privileged at a behind the scenes peek at something truly American, the great game of basketball.

Norman MacLean

Norb Ecksl

THE BASKETBALL QUIZBOOK

Chapter 1

PRO BASKETBALL'S EARLY DAYS / QUESTIONS

1. One of the earliest pro basketball teams was derived from a club which won the National A.A.U. title in 1897. What was this team called when it won the A.A.U. crown?
2. What pro squad did this A.A.U. title team become?
3. Another of the great early pro basketball clubs began as an amateur group of 14-year-olds from a major city in the Northeast. It later became one of the first teams admitted as a complete team to the Basketball Hall of Fame. What was this club called?
4. A famous early pro club, also admitted to the Basketball Hall of Fame *en masse*, was named for a dance hall in which it played most of its home games. Name the team.
5. A Troy, N.Y. team once broke the 111-game winning streak of a pro team far more famous than itself. Name the club which broke the streak.
6. Name the man who coached the most famous of all of the early all-Negro pro clubs based in New York.
7. This club started out as a barnstorming pro club and continued its existence giving comedy exhibitions. Name the team.
8. Name the only white player ever to wear the uniform of this team regularly.
9. The Original Celtics were one of the most fabled teams in the early history of pro basketball following their origination as the New York Celtics. Who started this team and when?
10. Two brothers reorganized the Celtics after the club had suspended operations. Name the brothers.
11. The Original Celtics met the New York Whirlwinds for the world basketball championship in 1921. Who won this best two-of-three series?
12. Two of the major stars of the Whirlwinds ultimately played for the Celtics. Name them.
13. Name the team which claimed the world title in 1922-23.
14. A team which originated in Schenectady, N.Y. subsequently became a famous touring pro club based in another New York State town. Name the team and the town.
15. This team was built around two brothers who later became noted college basketball coaches. Who were the brothers?
16. On November 11, 1941, at New York's Madison Square Garden, the Original Celtics played their final game. What team did they play against?
17. Name the two men generally acknowledged to be the best coaches produced from the Original Celtics. Both are members of the Basketball Hall of Fame.
18. One of the finest of the early pro players, this man was only 5' 4". After graduation from City College, he gained early recognition by playing for the New York Whirlwinds and later coached several pro clubs including the New York Gothams and the Brooklyn Jewels. Name him.
19. What famous singer and show business personality once sponsored the Original Celtics?
20. Who is known as the "Connie Mack of Pro Basketball"?

ANSWERS / PRO BASKETBALL'S EARLY DAYS

1. The club was known as the 23rd St. Y.M.C.A. of New York when it won the National A.A.U. title in 1897.
2. The 23rd St. Y.M.C.A. team later became the New York Wanderers.
3. The Buffalo (N.Y.) Germans.
4. The team was the New York Renaissance, so named for the Renaissance Ballroom where many of its games were played.
5. The Buffalo Germans' 111-game winning streak was broken in late 1910-11 by the 31st Separist Co. of Herkimer, N.Y.
6. Bobby Douglas was the coach of the New York Renaissance.
7. The Harlem Globetrotters, who have actually always been based in Chicago despite their name, started in 1925 as a barnstorming club.
8. Abe Saperstein, the founder and guiding light of the Globetrotters, was a player during the team's early seasons, mostly to save himself from paying a salary to another player.
9. The team later famed as the Original Celtics was formed as the New York Celtics in 1911-12 by Frank McCormack whose promotional efforts did much to increase coverage and interest in pro basketball.
10. Jim and Tom Furey reorganized the Celtics in 1918 and adopted the name Original Celtics.
11. Nobody won this series. The Whirlwinds took the opening game, played before 11,000 fans at the 71st Regiment Armory, and the Celtics evened the series by winning game two. The third and deciding game was never played.
12. The two Whirlwind stars who shifted over to the Celtics were Nat Holman and Chris Leonard.
13. The Kingston (N.Y.) Colonials claimed the world pro title in 1922-23 after defeating the Original Celtics in a five-game series.
14. The team which began as Co. E of Schenectady, N.Y., won the 1905 national championship by defeating the Kansas City Blue Diamonds. Later, the team became Co. G of Gloversville, N.Y., and, ultimately, the Troy Trojans based in Troy, N.Y. It was in Troy that they achieved their greatest stature once touring across the country and winning 29 straight games.
15. The two stars of the Troy Trojans were Ed and Lew Wachter.
16. The Celtics' final game was an exhibition against the New York Giants pro football club.
17. Although many of the Original Celtics became collegiate and pro coaches, the two best known were probably Joe Lapchick and Elmer Ripley. Nat Holman, who coached City College of New York to the famous double (N.C.A.A. and N.I.T.) victory in 1951 also played for the Celtics.
18. Barney Sedran, a 1911 graduate of C.C.N.Y., began a pro career after graduation which lasted as a player and coach until 1946. He was elected to the Basketball Hall of Fame in 1962.
19. Kate Smith owned the Celtics for two seasons and they were sometimes billed as the Kate Smith Celtics during those years.
20. Frank (Pop) Morgenweck is generally known as the "Connie Mack of Pro Basketball" in honor of his 32 years of coaching, financing and promoting the pro game. He operated teams in Philadelphia, Ft. Wayne, Pittsburgh, Rochester and Paterson, N.J., and coached the Chicago Bruins for George Halas. He is also credited with the discovery and development of such pro stars as Johnny Beckman, Benny Borgmann, Carl Husta and George Artus.

The Buffalo Germans as Champions in 1901. This picture was taken for the old archives of the Pros' Early Stages.

4 / PRO BASKETBALL'S EARLY DAYS

The present-day Celtics were preceded by some great players who made the team in the Old Days (1923). Left to right; Johnny Beckman, Johnny Whitty, Nat Holman, Jack Barry and Chris Leonard.

Nat Holman with the Celtics in 1926. Again an almost forgotten shot from the Pro's Early Years.

6 / PRO BASKETBALL'S EARLY DAYS

Can you recognize the late Johnny Beckman? He was not inducted into the Basketball Hall of Fame until 1974.

One of the Original Celtics, Joe Lapchick.

Chapter 2

NATIONAL BASKETBALL LEAGUE / QUESTIONS

1. What season did the National Basketball League start?
2. In the early years of the N.B.L., the dominant teams were Ohio-based clubs sponsored by two rubber companies. Name them.
3. Name the clubs that moved into the new N.B.A. when the National League merged into the Basketball Association of America.
4. One team was a charter member of the N.B.L., won several championships but did not shift into the N.B.A. during the merger. What was this team?
5. At the time it left the National League to join the B.A.A., one team was playing in the smallest-capacity arena in the B.A.A. Which team was it?
6. The N.B.L. once had a team named for one of the most famous military vehicles ever built. What was the team called and where was it based?
7. For many years, a club in the N.B.L. was owned by a local florist. What was his name and where was the team located?
8. One of the more startling upsets in the N.B.L.'s history occurred in the 1945-46 playoffs. What team won them?
9. Name the famous pro football player who was a member of a championship N.B.L. club.
10. One of the first "regional" franchises in pro sports was an N.B.L. club which represented cities in two states. What was the club called and what cities did it represent?
11. A midwest newspaperman was one of the key officials in the N.B.L. for many years. Name him.
12. What team did George Mikan begin his professional basketball career with?
13. A regular catcher with the St. Louis Cardinals played with the Rochester Royals during their N.B.L. years. Who was he?
14. What team won the last N.B.L. championship in 1948-49?
15. Who was the N.B.L. Rookie of the Year in 1948-49?
16. Only one team in the 12-year history of the N.B.L. won three straight league titles. What was the team and what years did it win the championships?
17. A University of Kentucky all-American and a University of Wisconsin star whose son later played for Wisconsin, carried their team to two straight N.B.L. titles. Name the team and the men.
18. What cities had teams in the N.B.L. at two different times, neither of which survived into the N.B.A.?
19. Name the man who led the N.B.L. in scoring during its first three seasons of operation.
20. What N.B.L. club played in the Edgerton Park Sports Arena?
21. What is the N.B.L. record for highest scoring average in a season and who holds it?
22. Name the first man to average over 20 points per game in an N.B.L. season.
23. Which N.B.L. charter-member team played every season of the league's existence?
24. How many teams began the first season of the N.B.L. in 1937-38?
25. What team led the N.B.L. in defeats in 1948-49 and achieved the same dubious distinction in the N.B.A. in 1949-50?
26. Name the two men who led the N.B.L. in scoring while playing on teams which won the league championship.

NATIONAL BASKETBALL LEAGUE / QUESTIONS

27. Name the only city to have two N.B.L. teams at the same time.
28. The team now known as the Atlanta Hawks in the N.B.A. began its existence as a National Basketball League club. It has played in four cities in the N.B.A. since 1949-50. What season did it begin in the National League and in what city?
29. What team won the most divisional and league championships during the 12-year history of the N.B.L.?
30. Although several teams currently in the N.B.A. trace their lineage to N.B.L. clubs of long vintage, several cities have had N.B.A. clubs unrelated to the N.B.L. teams which played in the same cities. Name four cities which have had teams in both the N.B.L. and N.B.A. at different times.
31. Originally the recreation director for the Zollner Piston Corporation, this man coached the Ft. Wayne Pistons to N.B.L. titles in 1943-44 and 1944-45. Name him.
32. An all-American selection from Texas A & M and an all-N.B.L. center, this man led the league in scoring in 1945-46 after his release from the service enabled him to rejoin Oshkosh. Name him.
33. Later coach of two N.B.A. teams, this former star for City College of New York was a regular guard on the Rochester championship N.B.L. team of 1945-46. Name him.
34. Name the lowest number of teams to compete in a full season of N.B.L. play and the year this occurred.
35. A noted all-American for St. John's of New York played part of his career with the Waterloo Hawks of the N.B.L. Who is he?
36. What is the N.B.L. record for most losses by a team in a season?
37. Name the man who later coached N.B.A. championship teams in St. Louis and Philadelphia after beginning his pro playing career with the Oshkosh All-Stars.
38. The coach of the Waterloo Hawks in 1948-49 was a member of the famous Ft. Wayne Zollner Piston club during World War II. Who is he?
39. A member of championship N.B.L. teams in both Oshkosh and Ft. Wayne, this man later played on a Baltimore N.B.A. title club and subsequently coached the Bullets as well. Name him.
40. Once during the 12-year history of the N.B.L., the league's individual scoring champion failed to average in double figures. Name the man and the year he achieved this odd distinction.
41. Who coached the Minneapolis Lakers to the 1947-48 N.B.L. title?
42. What team set the record for most victories in a single N.B.L. season and what year was the record set?
43. In its 12-year history, the N.B.L. had only three post-season championship playoff winners that did not win their respective division titles during the regular season. Which were the clubs that accomplished this feat and in what years was it done?
44. Match the names of the cities below with the nicknames for their N.B.L. teams:

    A) Sheboygan, Wisconsin   (1) Redskins
    B) Toledo, Ohio   (2) All-Stars
    C) Syracuse, N.Y.   (3) Hawks
    D) Waterloo, Iowa   (4) Bears
    E) Chicago, Ill.   (5) Jeeps
    F) Anderson, Ind.   (6) Nationals
    G) Oshkosh, Wisconsin   (7) American Gears
    H) Youngstown, Ohio   (8) Duffey Packers

45. The coach of the Hammond Buccaneers in 1948-49 was a playing coach who later was a high school basketball coach in Calumet City, Ill. He was a Notre Dame all-American. Name him.
46. Name two of the five men on the first team of the post-season all-star squad selected after the 1948-49 N.B.L. season and the teams for which they played.
47. Name the man who was released by Ft. Wayne in 1945 to become the coach of a competing N.B.L. team and later served as coach of the Pistons.
48. When the Ft. Wayne Pistons were formed in 1941, they signed two standouts from Indiana University as the backbone of their club. Name these two men.
49. A University of Wisconsin all-American was the star of the Sheboygan Redskins for several seasons. Who was he?
50. Name the Seton Hall all-American who starred with the Great Lakes Naval Training School team while in Naval Service during World War II, and who then became a star with the Rochester Royals of the N.B.L.

ANSWERS / NATIONAL BASKETBALL LEAGUE

1. The National Basketball League began competition in the 1937-38 season.
2. Two teams were based in Akron, O., and they were sponsored by the Goodyear and Firestone rubber Companies. Between them, they won the first three championships in N.B.L. history.
3. The clubs shifting into the new N.B.A. directly from the National League at the end of the 1948-49 season were the Sheboygan Redskins, Anderson Packers, Syracuse Nationals, Denver Nuggets, Waterloo Hawks, and Tri-Cities Blackhawks.
4. One of pro basketball's better-known teams at the time, the Oshkosh All-Stars, did not join the new N.B.A. when it was formed in the merger of the National League and the B.A.A. Instead, the All-Stars sought to provide a drive to reform the N.B.L., and an organization known as the National Professional Basketball League briefly resulted.
5. The Ft. Wayne Pistons. They played their games in the North Side High School Gymnasium in Ft. Wayne until the Coliseum was opened in 1952. The North Side H.S. Gym seated 3,800, the Coliseum 9,306.
6. The club was the Toledo Jeeps which was entered in the N.B.L. during World War II. Its best player was Chuck Chuckovitz.
7. The club was the Indianapolis team which was owned by Frank Kautsky and managed by Paul Walk; it was known for many years as the Kautskys, later as the Jets. It jumped to the B.A.A. in 1948.
8. The 1945-46 N.B.L. playoffs were won by the Rochester Royals, a new team playing its first season in the league. The semifinal round actually produced the biggest upset as the Royals beat defending champion Ft. Wayne, which had finished first in the Eastern Division. The Royals defeated Sheboygan in three straight games to win the playoff finals.
9. Otto Graham, famous quarterback of the Cleveland Browns, played for the Rochester Royals.
10. The Tri-Cities Blackhawks, owned by Ben Kerner of Buffalo. The Blackhawks played in the Wheaton Fieldhouse (capacity 6,000) in Moline, Ill.; they also represented Rock Island, Ill., and Davenport, Iowa.
11. Leo Fisher of the Chicago Herald American, a Hearst-owned afternoon newspaper, was the driving force behind the N.B.L. for many years.
12. After graduating from DePaul University, Mikan began his pro career with the Chicago American Gears. After they folded, he moved to the Minneapolis Lakers for the 1947-48 season and created a dynasty with the Lakers.
13. Del Rice played with the Rochester Royals' N.B.L. championship team of 1945-46. He was a regular catcher with the St. Louis Cardinals from 1945 to 1955 and also played with the Milwaukee Braves, Chicago Cubs, Baltimore Orioles and L.A. Angels before ending his big-league career in 1961.
14. The last N.B.L. championship was won by the Anderson Packers in 1948-49. The team was based in Anderson, Indiana and was owned by Ike W. Duffey, who also happened to be the president of the N.B.L. at the time of the merger between the N.B.L. and the B.A.A. into the N.B.A.
15. Dolph Schayes of the Syracuse Nationals was the N.B.L. Rookie of the Year in 1948-49 after graduating from New York University.
16. The club which won three straight N.B.L. titles was the Ft. Wayne Pistons. They turned the trick in 1942-43, 1943-44, and 1944-45.

ANSWERS / NATIONAL BASKETBALL LEAGUE / 13

17. The two stars of the Oshkosh All-Stars were LeRoy Edwards of the University of Kentucky and Gene Englund of Wisconsin, Englund's son played for the Badgers two decades later.
18. Hammond, Indiana, had teams twice in the N.B.L. and so did Dayton, O. Hammond's first club, known as the Caesars (or Caesar's Pros), was owned by a local automobile dealer and played from 1938-39 to 1940-41. The second, nicknamed the Buccaneers, was a community-owned team in 1948-49. Dayton had a club in only the first (1937-38) and last (1948-49) years of the league. The second club was really the New York Renaissance Five transplanted to Dayton to replace the Detroit Gems who folded during the 1948-49 season.
19. LeRoy Edwards of Oshkosh was the N.B.L. scoring leader in 1937-38 (16.1 points per game), 1938-39 (11.9), and 1939-40 (9.0).
20. The Rochester Royals played in the Edgerton Park Sports Arena (capacity 5,000) from 1945-46 until 1954-55 when they moved into the War Memorial Auditorium opened in 1955.
21. The N.B.L. record for highest scoring average is 21.3 points per game set by George Mikan of the Minneapolis Lakers in 1947-48.
22. Mel Riebe of Cleveland was the first man in the N.B.L. to average over 20 points per game with 20.2 in 1944-45.
23. The Oshkosh All-Stars were members of the N.B.L. from 1937-38 to 1948-49, compiling an overall record of 227-158.
24. A total of 13 teams were members of the N.B.L. during its initial season of 1937-38. They were the Akron Goodyears, Oshkosh Ft. Wayne, Whiting (Ind.), Indianapolis, Cincinnati, Dayton, Kankakee, the Akron Firestones, Pittsburgh, Buffalo, Warran (Pa.) and Columbus (O.).
25. The Denver Nuggets, an amateur team turned pro, had the worst record in the N.B.L. (18-44) in 1948-49, and posted the same kind of mark with an 11-51 season in the N.B.A. in 1949-50, after which the team disbanded.
26. In 12 years, only Bob McDermott of Ft. Wayne (1942-43) and George Mikan of Minneapolis (1947-48) won scoring titles while playing on N.B.L. championship teams.
27. Akron, Ohio had two N.B.L. clubs simultaneously from 1937-38 to 1940-41, when the Firestones folded at the end of season. The Goodyears called it quits after the next season.
28. The club now known as the Atlanta Hawks started in Buffalo in 1946, moved to Moline, Ill. midway through the 1946-47 season, next became the Tri-Cities Blackhawks, then the Milwaukee Hawks in 1951, the St. Louis Hawks in 1955, and the Atlanta Hawks in 1968.
29. Oshkosh won five Western Division titles and two outright league championships in 12 seasons, including three straight Western titles followed by two league crowns from 1937-38 to 1941-42.
30. Actually, there are six cities which have had unrelated teams in both the N.B.L. and N.B.A. at different times. They are Buffalo, Cleveland, Chicago and Detroit, which currently have N.B.A. clubs, and Pittsburgh and Cincinnati, which have had teams in both the N.B.L. and N.B.A. or B.A.A. at different times but do not now have a pro basketball club.
31. Carl Bennett was the coach of the Pistons in the war-time championship years and was initially instrumental in encouraging Ft. Wayne owner Fred Zollner to join the N.B.L.

32. Bob Carpenter was the Oshkosh center who led the N.B.L. in scoring in 1945-46 with a 13.9 average, 442 points in 32 games.
33. William (Red) Holzman, later coach of the Milwaukee Hawks and New York Knickerbockers in the N.B.A., played for the Rochester Royals when they won the N.B.L. title in 1945-46.
34. In 1943-44, the N.B.L. operated with only four teams (Ft. Wayne, Oshkosh, Sheboygan and Cleveland).
35. Harry Boykoff was the former St. John's of New York all-American who played for the Waterloo Hawks of the N.B.L.
36. The N.B.L. record for most losses by a team in a season was set by the Flint Dows of Flint, Mich. in 1947-48 when they lost 52 of 60 games.
37. Alex Hannun, a graduate of the University of Southern California, broke into pro basketball with the Oshkosh All-Stars in 1948-49.
38. Charles Shipp, purchased by Ft. Wayne from Oshkosh in 1943, coached the Waterloo Hawks.
39. Buddy Jeanette, a 1938 graduate of Washington & Jefferson College, played at Oshkosh and Ft. Wayne before joining Baltimore.
40. LeRoy Edwards of Oshkosh won the N.B.L. scoring title in 1939-40 with an average of 9.0 points per game.
41. Johnny Kundla who guided the club to championships in 1947-48 in the N.B.L., in 1948-49 in the B.A.A. and to N.B.A. championships in 1949-50, 1951-52, 1952-53 and 1953-54.
42. Anderson won the most games in a single season in 1948-49 when the Packers captured the Eastern Division title with 49 wins in 64 games.
43. The three teams which won the playoff championship without finishing first in their division were the Akron Goodyears in 1937-38 (second in the East), the Rochester Royals in 1945-46 (second in the East), and the Chicago Gears in 1946-47 (fourth in the Western Division).
44. The nicknames match up with the cities as follows: (A) Sheboygan (1) Redskins, (B) Toledo (5) Jeeps, (C) Syracuse (6) Nationals, (D) Waterloo (3) Hawks, (E) Chicago (7) American Gears, (F) Anderson (8) Duffey Packers, (G) Oshkosh (2) All-Stars, and (H) Youngstown (4) Bears.
45. George Sobek, a guard, was the playing coach of the Hammond Buccaneers in 1948-49 and later coached at Thornton Fractional High School in Calumet City, Ill.
46. The first-team all-star squad selected after the 1948-49 N.B.L. was composed of Dick Mehen of Waterloo, Frank Brian of Anderson, Al Cervi of Syracuse, Don Otten of Tri-Cities, and Gene Englund of Oshkosh.
47. Paul Birch was released by Ft. Wayne to become the coach of the Youngstown Bears in 1945-46, moved to the Pittsburgh Ironmen of the B.A.A. in 1946-47, and later coached the Pistons for three seasons beginning in 1951-52.
48. Paul Armstrong and Herman Schaeffer were the two Indiana University stars signed by the Pistons as the nucleus for the first Ft. Wayne N.B.L. club in November, 1941.
49. Johnny Katz was the University of Wisconsin all-American who was the outstanding star for the Sheboygan Redskins.
50. Bob Davies, probably the finest ball-handler in N.B.L. history, was the star at Great Lakes before joining Rochester.

Chapter 3

OTHER LEAGUES / QUESTIONS

1. The first pro basketball league was formed in 1898. What was it called?
2. The first playoff in pro basketball history was won by a New York team in 1901. Who did they beat and what league were they in?
3. The Hudson River League lasted only three seasons, 1909-10 through 1911-12. One team won the title the only two years it was a league member. Name the team.
4. Pittston won the championship of a new pro league in 1914-15. What was the league called?
5. The original Eastern League was established in 1909-10. What team won the championship in the first season?
6. In the original Eastern League, a famous star in later years for the Original Celtics won the scoring title in 1920-21. Name him and his team.
7. What team won the championship of the Eastern League in its final season (1921-22) and how did they do it?
8. Over a six-year period, this famous team won five titles in six seasons in two different leagues. Name the team and the leagues. Hint: the period was 1909-10 to 1914-15.
9. What year was the New York State League established and how many seasons did it last?
10. What city once had its own complete professional basketball league?
11. A team once forfeited its chance to win a league championship by refusing to play the post-season playoffs. Name the team and the league.
12. Barney Sedran, one of pro basketball's most famous early stars, led his team to the New York State League title in 1920-21. What city was the team representing?
13. In 1922-23, the New York State League's playoff between the winning teams of both halves of the split schedule was cancelled. Why?
14. What two teams played in the championship playoffs during the first season of the original American Basketball League?
15. The American League had eight franchises in its first season, all of them to later have teams in one or more other major basketball leagues. Name five of the cities.
16. For three seasons, one city had teams in both the American League and the new Basketball Association of America. Name the city and the teams.
17. Name the famous major league baseball player who also played for the Brooklyn Gothams of the American League.
18. Who was the coach of the New York Gothams of the American League in 1945-46?
19. One team won the championships of the American League and the Basketball Association of America within a three-year period. What was the team?
20. What team won the last three championships of the American League?
21. A league still active began play in 1961-62. What is the league called and who is the long-time commissioner of the circuit?

ANSWERS / OTHER LEAGUES

1. The National League. Starting in 1898-99, the league lasted five seasons. The teams the first year included Trenton, Millville, Camden, Germantown, Philadelphia and Hancock.
2. New York defeated Trenton in two straight games after the two teams tied for the National League title in 1900-01.
3. The team was the Troy Trojans of Troy, N.Y., which included the Wachter brothers, Ed and Lew, and Chief Muller.
4. The Pennsylvania State League. Later including such cities as Scranton and Wilkes-Barre, the league lasted until 1920-21.
5. Trenton, led by Harry Hough and Charles Klein, won the first Eastern League championship in 1909-10.
6. The Eastern League scoring champion for 1920-21 was Nat Holman of Germantown who averaged 8.4 points per game, 285 points in 34 games.
7. The New York Celtics won the title of the Eastern League in 1921-22 by defeating Trenton in the playoffs, 2 games to 1, by scores of 24-20, a 22-17 defeat, and 27-22.
8. The Troy (N.Y.) Trojans won the Hudson River League title in 1909-10 and 1910-11, the New York State title in 1911-12, 1912-13 and 1914-15. They finished second in the N.Y.S.L. in 1913-14 by a single game behind Utica, N.Y.
9. The New York State League was set up in 1911-12 and lasted until 1922-23.
10. Philadelphia once had its own complete pro basketball league. The Philadelphia League, which included teams from nearby suburban towns, functioned for three years from 1903-04 to 1905-06. Jack Reynolds won the scoring title in 1904-05 with a strong 15.8 average in 39 games, scoring 616 points on 78 baskets and 460 free throws. The rules of basketball at that time provided for one man to shoot all of the free throws for his team.
11. Gloversville, N.Y. forfeited a chance to win the New York State League title in 1921-22 after taking the first-half crown in the regular season when it refused to play Cohoes, N.Y., the second-half winner, in the post-season playoffs.
12. Barney Sedran played for the Albany team which won the N.Y.S.L. title in 1920-21, and he was also the league scoring champion with an 8.4 average per game.
13. The post-season playoff between the winners of the two halves of the 1922-23 N.Y.S.L. schedule was cancelled because Kingston won both halves.
14. The two finishes in the playoffs at the end of the first American League season in 1926-27 were the Original Celtics and the Cleveland Rosenblums. The Celtics won the set in three straight games.
15. The eight franchises in the American League in 1926-27 were New York (Original Celtics), Cleveland, Ft. Wayne, Rochester, Chicago, Washington, Philadelphia and Baltimore.
16. The city which had both A.L. and B.A.A. teams was Philadelphia. From 1946-47 to 1948-49 the A.L. was represented by the Sphas at Convention Hall, and the B.A.A. by the Warriors at the Philadelphia Arena.
17. Pete Reiser, star outfielder for the Brooklyn Dodgers and a National League batting champion, also played for the Brooklyn Gothams of the American League in pro basketball.

18. Barney Sedran was the New York Gothams' coach in 1945-46. With the arrival of the Knickerbockers and the powerful backing by them of Madison Square Garden in 1946-47, the Gothams shifted to Brooklyn before expiring in 1949.
19. The Baltimore Bullets accomplished the unique feat of winning the A.L. title in 1945-46, taking the regular season title of the A.L. in 1946-47 and winning the B.A.A. championship in 1947-48 after jumping from the A.L.
20. The last three championships of the old American League were won by the Scranton (Pa.) Miners in 1949-50, 1950-51 and 1951-52.
21. The league started in 1961-62 was called the Eastern Professional Basketball League and is now known as the E.P.B.A.; its long-time commissioner is Harry Rudolph, father of ex-N.B.A. ref Mendy.

18 / OTHER LEAGUES

Marques Haynes in 1951

Goose Tatum

Chapter 4

AMERICAN BASKETBALL LEAGUE / QUESTIONS

1. When was the American Basketball League formed and what world-famous team was responsible for its formation? The team was never a member of the league.
2. Who was the owner of the Chicago franchise in the ABL and what was the team's nickname?
3. A famous player was blacklisted by the NBA and signed with the ABL. Who was he and why was he blacklisted?
4. The New York franchise of the ABL was originally an amateur team which, with some player additions, moved into the neophyte pro league. What was it called and why?
5. A former St. John's star coached in the ABL and later became a coach in the NBA. What ABL team did he coach and who was he?
6. Who was the owner of the Cleveland club in the ABL and what famous college all-American did he attempt to sign before the league folded?
7. A member of the New York Knicks jumped the NBA and joined a team in the ABL to be closer to his home and the area where he attended college. Who was he?
8. What team did this man join in the ABL?
9. When the ABL was formed it had a team outside of the continental United States. Where was this team located and what was it called?
10. Who was the scoring champion of the ABL in 1960-61?
11. One of the original coaches in the ABL was a former all-star with the Boston Celtics and later a famous NBA coach. Who is he?
12. Name the five members of the All-League ABL team for the 1960-61 season.
13. Kansas City was defeated in the ABL playoff finals in 1961 by the team which won the first league championship. Name the winning team.
14. In its second, and final season (1962-63) the ABL shrunk down to six teams and failed to finish its schedule. Which team won the championship that season?
15. What man led the ABL in scoring in 1962-63 and who did he play for?
16. What was commonly known as the New York franchise in the ABL began the 1961-62 season in Washington before shifting to New York. Where did it play in 1962-63?
17. A famous player from the University of Kentucky who was involved in the 1951 college basketball scandal became one of the leading scorers in the ABL. Name him.
18. A team in the ABL in 1962-63 had the same nickname as the minor league baseball club from the same city which was once managed by Casey Stengel. What was the team and the city?
19. The championship team in the ABL in 1961-62 didn't play in the league the following season. Why?
20. The ABL pioneered a rule which was later adopted by the American Basketball Association when the ABA began competition in 1967. What was the rule?

ANSWERS / AMERICAN BASKETBALL LEAGUE

1. The American Basketball League was formed in 1960, and the 1960-61 season proved to be its only full season of operation. The Harlem Globetrotters provided the principal funding for the ABL, although they never participated in an official ABL game, being too valuable as an independent attraction. The Globies appeared frequently as preliminary bookings to ABL games, especially in the weaker cities (which were numerous). As a result of their backing of the competitive league, many NBA clubs stopped booking the Globetrotters in their arenas for several years, even after the ABL went out of existence.
2. Abe Saperstein, owner of the Globetrotters, was the owner of the Chicago club which was nicknamed the Majors. Among the stars of the Majors were Tony Jackson, a former St. John's all-American, and Ron Zagar of Iowa. Saperstein picked the Chicago club as his team even though, as the principal backer of the ABL, he had his choice of cities, because of the fact that the Globetrotters, altough named for Harlem, have always been based in Chicago.
3. Connie Hawkins was the man. A fabulously famous high school player at Boys High in Brooklyn, Hawkins matriculated to Iowa and was blacklisted by the NBA for alleged consorting with known gamblers anf for failure to report an alleged bribe offer. Hawkins subsequently sued the NBA and was allowed to play. In the ABL he played for the Pittsburgh Rens.
4. Originally one of the industrial teams in Amateur Athletic Union competition, the Tuck Tapers shifted into the ABL in 1960-61. The team was known as the Tuck Tapers because it was owned by the Technical Tape Company of New Rochelle, N.Y., whose president, Paul Cohen, was also president of the team. When it was an amateur club, the Tuck Tapers played in New York's 69th Regiment Armory. When they turned pro, the club had to move to the Long Island Arena in Commack. Unable to succeed there, it was ultimately moved to Washington, D.C.
5. Jack McMahon, later coach of the Cincinnati Royals, was coach of the Kansas City club in the ABL.
6. George Steinbrenner, chief executive of the American Shipbuilding Company, was the owner of the Cleveland club in the ABL and he actively sought to sign Jerry Lucas, then an Ohio State all-American, before the ABL collapsed. Steinbrenner later became principal owner of the New York Yankees and was suspended from his position with the Yankees after being convicted of Federal election campaign law violations. Steinbrenner has also been active as a co-producer of Broadway theatrical shows.
7. Kenny Sears who played college ball at Santa Clara.
8. The San Francisco Saints.
9. One of the charter members of the ABL was based in Honolulu and was known as the Hawaii Chiefs. After winning only 29 and losing 53 in 1961-62, the club was shifted to Long Beach, Calif. for the 1962-63 season.
10. Connie Hawkins of Pittsburgh who averaged 27.5 points per game.
11. Bill Sharman coached the Los Angeles Jets. After the Jets folded on January 18, 1962, he shifted to Cleveland and coached the Pipers.
12. The five first-team All-Stars were Hawkins, Dan Swartz of New York, Bill Bridges and Larry Staverman of Kansas City and Dick Barnett of Cleveland.

13. Cleveland defeated Kansas City, 3 games to 2, to win the only ABL championship playoff series ever held.
14. The Kansas City Steers were in first place with a 22-9 record (3½ games ahead of Long Beach) on December 31, 1962, when the ABL collapsed, and they were awarded the de facto league championship.
15. Bill Bridges averaged 29.2, appearing in 29 of the 31 games played by the Kansas City Steers. Bridges had 849 points on 312 baskets and 225 free throws, leading ABL scorers in all three departments.
16. The New York Tapers were moved to Philadelphia for the 1962-63 season, filling a void in the Quaker City left by the departure of the Warriors to San Francisco. After the ABL folded, the Syracuse Nationals of the NBA moved to Philadelphia and became the 76ers.
17. Bill Spivey, one of the "point-shavers" of 1951, was second in ABL scoring in 1961-62 and third in 1962-63 while playing for the Hawaii (later Long Beach) Chiefs. He was a 7-foot center with a deadly hook shot from 15-to-18 feet out.
18. The Oakland Oaks. The name was later adopted by an original ABA team which starred Rick Barry and was coached by Bruce Hale.
19. The Cleveland Pipers were promised an NBA franchise for 1962-63 if they could sign Jerry Lucas. When Lucas signed with Cincinnati of the NBA, the Pipers were left out of both leagues.
20. The 3-point basket from beyond the 25-foot circle.

Chapter 5

NATIONAL BASKETBALL ASSOCIATION (PLAYERS) / QUESTIONS

1. The individual record for most points in a game is held by Wilt Chamberlain. How many points did he score and what team was the playing for when he accomplished this feat?
2. When Chamberlain set the record for an N.B.A. game, who was the opposition and where was the game played?
3. At the time he set the record, what was the previous high single-game individual point total in N.B.A. history?
4. How many different men have scored over 70 points in an N.B.A. game? Name them.
5. How many different men have scored over 60 points in an N.B.A. game? Name them.
6. Only two of these men turned the trick of 60 or more points in a single game prior to the introduction of the 24-second rule. Who are they?
7. What is the individual record for most field goals made in an N.B.A. game and who holds the record?
8. Which of these men was the first to crack the 60-point barrier in a single game and when did he do it?
9. What is the record for the most free throws made by an individual in a game?
10. Although Bill Russell is generally acknowledged to be the finest rebounder in the history of the pro game, the record for most rebounds in a game is held by another man who, oddly, set the record *against* the Celtics. What is the record and who holds it?
11. A Celtic and a Warrior are the co-holders of the N.B.A. mark for most assists in a single game. Who are they and what is the record total?
12. One man exceeded 30,000 points in his N.B.A. career. Name him.
13. Eight men have crossed the 20,000-point mark in their N.B.A. careers including games played through 1975. Name them.
    Hint: two of them were teammates on the same club for ten years.
14. Name the first man ever to score over 2,000 points in an N.B.A. season and the team he played for.
15. The first man to score over 3,000 points in a single season also was the first to top the 4,000-point level in a season. Name him.
16. What was Wilt Chamberlain's points-per-game average in 1961-62?
17. How many men have won two or more N.B.A. scoring championships in succession? Name them.
18. Name the only men ever to win the N.B.A. scoring crown in two non-successive seasons and the teams they played for when the feats were accomplished.
19. Who was the first scoring champion of the N.B.A. as it is presently structured?
20. From 1952-53 to 1961-62 only two men led the N.B.A. in foul-shooting accuracy. Name the two and the number of times each led the league during this span.
21. One man twice achieved the statistical oddity of leading the league in scoring and most personal fouls. Name him.

NATIONAL BASKETBALL ASSOCIATION (PLAYERS) / QUESTIONS

22. Who set the original "iron man" record for consecutive games in the N.B.A.?
23. Who holds the record for fouling out of the most games in a single season and who did he play for?
24. What man set the record for most personal fouls in a single season?
25. What man played the most games in a career without ever fouling out of a game and how many games did he play?
26. Who holds the record for the most assists per game in a season and when was the record set?
27. No man has ever played every minute of every game his team played in an N.B.A. season. Who came the closest? When?
28. What is the record for the most successive free throws made in a single game and who holds it?
29. What is the N.B.A. record for most consecutive games of over 50 points by a player and who holds it?
30. Who holds the record for the most personal fouls on one man in a single game and what was his total?
31. What do Connie Dierking, Henry Akin, Bud Ogden and Don Smith have in common?
32. Twice in N.B.A. history a man has scored 13 points in a 5-minute overtime period. Who did it?
33. Bill Sharman, great foul shooter and playmaker for the Celtics, holds the record for the most free throws made in succession in regular season N.B.A. play. How many in a row did he make?
34. At the start of the 1975-76 season, there were six men named Smith on the veteran rosters of N.B.A. clubs. Name them and their respective teams.
35. One N.B.A. player once scored 32 straight points without missing a single shot either from the floor or the foul line. Who achieved this remarkable streak?
36. Although they were charter members of the league, the New York Knickerbockers didn't have their first man named to the N.B.A. All-Star team at the end of the season until 1953-54. Who was the first Knick named?
37. What man was the leading scorer on his N.B.A. team one season and was coach of the team the following season as an non-player?
38. What do the following N.B.A. players have in common: Ray Felix, Walt Bellamy, Jerry Lucas and Earl Monroe?
39. What former N.B.A. player had a sister who was a Miss America?
40. Which former N.B.A. player is married to a former Miss America?
41. Who was the last member of the Fort Wayne Pistons to earn a berth on the first-team N.B.A. All-Star squad at the end of the season?
42. One man led the N.B.A. in fouling out of games for four straight seasons. Name him.
43. What man once scored 15 straight points in an N.B.A. game without any other player on either team scoring a single point?
44. Who was the last player-coach in the N.B.A. to lead his team to a championship?
45. What high-scoring N.B.A. forward became nationally known for his work to assist another player who was crippled by illness?
46. Two men in N.B.A. history have scored 12 field goals in a single quarter. Name them.

47. Red Auerbach became famous as the coach and architect of the Boston Celtic dynasty. What other team did he coach to a regular-season Eastern Division title?
48. What N.B.A. referee also coached a team in the league after he quit officiating?
49. One N.B.A. coach also coached the same college team to championships in the National Invitational Tournament before and after his N.B.A. coaching career. Name him.
50. Red Auerbach was the third man to serve as coach of the Boston Celtics. Name his two predecessors, both of whom left the Celtics to have successful college coaching careers.
51. Only three men have served as commissioners of the N.B.A. in the 30-year history of the league. Name them.
52. One N.B.A. commissioner had to resign an elected office to accept the job. Who was he and what job did he resign?
53. Two brothers owned and operated the Royals' franchise throughout its entire history in Rochester. Name them.
54. Who holds the N.B.A. record for the most free throws made in his career?
55. The record for most games played in an N.B.A. career is 1,122. Who holds this record?
56. Seven men in N.B.A. history have accumulated more than 3,000 personal fouls in their careers. Name any three of them.
57. What man played the most seasons in the N.B.A. and what team did he play for?
58. Name three men who played in the N.B.A. and also in the baseball major leagues.
59. On 13 occasions in N.B.A. history, a team has had two men collect 1,000 or more rebounds in the same season. The Bullets have turned the trick more than any team, five times. Four of those pairs have included the same man as one of the rebounding aces. Name him.
60. A long-time N.B.A. referee also operated a flower shop in New York City. Name him.
61. The N.B.A. record for rebounds in a single season is 2,149. Name the man who achieved the record and the year he did it.
62. Who holds the record for the most assists by a player in a season and who did he play for when he set the record?
63. Who is the only N.B.A. Rookie-of-the-Year ever to lead the league in scoring in his rookie year?
64. This all-time superstar in pro basketball was drafted by a team which immediately traded him to another club. When that team went out of business before the season, he was chosen by a third club in a distribution lottery in which he was the last of three choices taken. He was won by a team which could have had him as a choice originally but didn't want him. Who is this great name in pro basketball history?
65. Over the periof from 1956-57 to 1968-69 only two coaches won N.B.A. championships. Red Auerbach won 11 titles in those 13 years with the Boston Celtics. Name the coach who won the other two titles and the teams he won them with.
66. In 1972-73 the Philadelphia 76ers compiled the worst record in N.B.A. history, finishing the season with a total of 9 wins and 73 losses. The 76ers were coached by two men that season, neither of whom returned the following year. Name them.

NATIONAL BASKETBALL ASSOCIATION (PLAYERS) / QUESTIONS

67. The Poldoloff Cup is awarded at the end of every N.B.A. season to the man selected as the Most Valuable Player in the league. One man won the award five times. Name him.
68. Name the backcourt men who have led the N.B.A. in fieldgoal shooting percentage.
69. Who was the first black player signed by an N.B.A. club? Hint: he was signed by the Boston Celtics.
70. A referee was once barred from the N.B.A. because of allegations that he had accepted $3,000 to alter the outcome of league games played during the 1950 season. Name him.
71. An N.B.A. clubowner was responsible for the introduction of the 24-second rule. Name him and the club of which he was the president.
72. The men who rank second and fourth respectively in all-time career scoring in the N.B.A. never led the league in points in a season. Name these two all-time all-stars.
73. At the start of the 1954-55 season three N.B.A. clubs were owned by the men who coached the team. Name these three owner-coaches and their clubs.
74. Name the first man to lead the N.B.A. in field goal percentage and scoring in the same season. Hint: he was a Warrior.
75. The Warriors, in Philadelphia and San Francisco, have won a total of 11 individual scoring titles. Four men account for this total. Name them.

ANSWERS / NATIONAL BASKETBALL ASSOCIATION

1. For most points in a single game the record is of course the 100 scored by Chamberlain while playing for the Philadelphia Warriors on March 2, 1962. He scored 59 points in the second half, 31 of them in the fourth quarter, and hit 100 points with 42 seconds to play in the game.
2. Chamberlain accomplished the record scoring spree against the New York Knickerbockers at Hershey, Pa., where the Warriors played several games each season during the years they were based in Philadelphia's Convention Hall. The Knicks' center was Darrell Imhoff.
3. The record which was broken that night by Chamberlain was his own mark of 78 set on December 8, 1961, against Los Angeles in a triple overtime game at Philadelphia.
4. Only two. Chamberlain (who did it 5 times and hit an even 70 once for good measure) and Elgin Baylor, who scored 71 against New York in Madison Square Garden on November 15, 1960.
5. Just five. Chamberlain, Baylor, Joe Fulks, Jerry West and George Mikan. Chamberlain did it 29 times, Baylor three and the others once each.
6. Fulks (in 1949) and Mikan (in 1952).
7. The record is 36, scored by Chamberlain in the same game against the Knicks at Hershey, Pa.
8. Joe Fulks of the Philadelphia Warriors was the first man ever to crack the 60-point barrier. He did it on February 10, 1949, against Indianapolis at Philadelphia with 27 field goals and 9 free throws. At the time, his performance was a stunning sports achievement and established a record which stood for a full decade until broken by Baylor, then with the Minneapolis Lakers, against the Boston Celtics on November 8, 1959, with 64 points at Minneapolis.
9. Chamberlain's 28 free throws in the game against the Knicks at Hershey is the record, but the best performance at the foul line in N.B.A. history may well have been Frank Selvy's effort of 24 out of 26 tries for Milwaukee against Minneapolis at Ft. Wayne on December 2, 1954. Chamberlain had 32 attempts to make his 28.
10. Surprise. Chamberlain holds this record, too. He grabbed 55 caroms against Boston on November 24, 1960, at Philadelphia. But the next three highest rebounding games belong to Bill Russell (51 and 49 twice).
11. The record is shared by Guy Rodgers and Bob Cousy, two of the finest playmakers in pro history. Cousy had 28 against Minneapolis on February 27, 1959, at Boston and Rodgers got 28 against St. Louis on March 14, 1963, at San Francisco.
12. Wilt Chamberlain scored 31,419 points in his 14-year N.B.A. career from 1960 through 1973.
13. Chamberlain, of course, scored over 20,000 points and so did: Oscar Robertson (second in career scoring with 26,710 points), the two teammates Elgin Baylor and Jerry West, John Havlicek, Hal Greer, Walt Bellamy and Bob Pettit.
14. The first man to score over 2,000 points in a single season was George Yardley, an aerodynamics engineer who played with the Ft. Wayne Pistons. He scored 2,001 points in 1957-58, getting his final two points on a layup after a steal in the final game of the year against the Syracuse Nationals.

15. Wilt Chamberlain scored 3,033 points in 1960-61, becoming the first man ever to turn the trick, and then set the all-time record of 4,029 points the following season. He played 79 games in 1960-61 and 80 in 1961-62.
16. Chamberlain averaged 50.4 points in 80 games in 1961-62.
17. Only five. Chamberlain, George Mikan, Neil Johnston of the Philadelphia Warriors, Lew Alcindor (Kareem Abdul-Jabbar), and Bob McAdoo. Chamberlain won seven straight scoring titles from 1959-60 to 1965-66.
18. The two men who have done this are Paul Arizin of the Philadelphia Warriors (1951-52 and 1956-57) and Bob Pettit of the St. Louis Hawks (1955-56 and 1958-59).
19. George Mikan in 1949-50.
20. The pair who became noted for their duels in free-throw accuracy were Bill Sharman of the Boston Celtics and Dolph Schayes of the Syracuse Nationals. During the years from 1952-53 to 1961-62, Sharman led the N.B.A. in accuracy seven times and Schaves three times.
21. George Mikan did it twice, 1949-50 and 1950-51.
22. Johnny Kerr of the Syracuse Nationals played 844 straight games from October 31, 1954, to November 4, 1965.
23. Don Meineke fouled out of 26 of the 69 games played by the Fort Wayne Pistons in 1952-53.
24. Bill Bridges accumulated 366 personals in 1967-68 for the St. Louis Hawks.
25. Wilt Chamberlain played his entire career of 1,045 games with Philadelphia, San Francisco and Los Angeles without ever fouling out of a game.
26. Oscar Robertson of the Cincinnati Royals averaged 11.5 assists per game in 1964-65.
27. Wilt Chamberlain came the closest, playing every minute of 79 of the 80 games during the 1961-62 season for the Philadelphia Warriors. Chamberlain logged a staggering 3,882 minutes of action that year and actually averaged 48.5 minutes per game or half a minute more than the regulation length of an N.B.A. game because he played so many minutes of overtime. Still, the Warriors finished second in the N.B.A. East to Syracuse.
28. The record is 19 straight set by Bob Pettit of the St. Louis Hawks against the Celtics at the Boston Garden on November 22, 1961.
29. In 1961-62 Wilt Chamberlain scored 50 or more points in 45 straight games.
30. Don Otten of the Tri-Cities Blackhawks was charged with eight personal fouls in a game against the Sheboygan Redskins on November 24, 1949, when his team ran out of players.
31. They are the four men in N.B.A. history who managed to acquire six personal fouls and get disqualified from a game in a single period.
32. The hot-shooting pair are Earl Monroe and Joe Caldwell. Strangely, though the feat has been accomplished only twice in the entire history of the N.B.A., Monroe and Caldwell did it within 12 days of each other in February, 1970, Monroe for Baltimore against Detroit and Caldwell for Atlanta against Cincinnati.
33. Sharman once sank 55 straight foul shots in 1956 during games from November 22 to December 27. In the 1959 playoff series, he was even more remarkable, making 56 in a row from the charity stripe.
34. Bobby (Bingo) Smith of Cleveland, Don Smith of Philadelphia, Elmore Smith of Los Angeles, Greg Smith of Portland, Phil Smith of Golden State and Randy Smith of Buffalo.

ANSWERS / NATIONAL BASKETBALL ASSOCIATION

35. Larry Costello of the Syracuse Nationals made 13 baskets and 6 free throws on December 8, 1961, before finally missing a shot.
36. Harry Gallatin was the first Knick chosen for the N.B.A. All-Star club picked officially by writers and broadcasters at the end of the season.
37. Bobby Wanzer of the Rochester Royals led the club in scoring with a 13.1 average in 1954-55 and was named coach in 1955-56. He served as coach for three seasons and part of 1958-59 before being relieved by Tom Marshall after the Royals had moved to Cincinnati.
38. All four were chosen N.B.A. Rookie-of-the-Year for different teams but ultimately spent parts of their careers with the New York Knickerbockers. Felix was chosen in 1954 playing for Baltimore, Bellamy in 1962 with Chicago, Lucas for Cincinnati in 1964 and Monroe in 1968 for Baltimore.
39. Mel Hutchins who played with the Pistons in the late 1950's and early 1960's. His sister, Colleen Kay Hutchins, was chosen Miss America in 1952.
40. Dr. Ernie Vandeweghe, a former Knick, married Kay Hutchins.
41. Larry Fouts, a center from LaSalle, was a first-time All-Star in 1955-56. The Pistons moved to Detroit two seasons later.
42. Walter Dukes while playing for Detroit led the N.B.A. in disqualifications each year from 1958-59 to 1961-62, hitting a high of 22 games in 1959-60.
43. Wilt Chamberlain scored 15 straight points in a game at the Baltimore Civic Center on March 20, 1966, while playing for the Philadelphia Warriors.
44. Bill Russell.
45. Jack Twyman of the Royals (Rochester and Cincinnati), who twice finished as runner-up in scoring (1958-59 to Bob Pettit and 1959-60 to Wilt Chamberlain), later became a television broadcaster and was most noted for his efforts to aid stricken former teammate Maurice Stokes.
46. Cliff Hagan of the St. Louis Hawks against the Knicks at Madison Square Garden on February 4, 1958, and Chamberlain in his 100-point game at Hershey, Pa., on March 2, 1962.
47. Auerbach coached the original Washington Capitals in 1946-47 and the club finished with a 49-11 record, first in the Eastern Division, but was eliminated in the semifinals of the playoffs by Chicago, the Western Division champion.
48. Charlie Eckman refereed in the N.B.A. before he became the coach of the Pistons in 1954. He was replaced as Detroit coach in 1958 by Red Rocha and had a long and colorful career as a collegiate referee thereafter.
49. Joe Lapchick coached the Knickerbockers from 1947-48 to 1955-56. He also coached St. John's University to N.I.T. titles in 1943, 1944, 1959 and 1965.
50. John (Honey) Russell was the first Celtic coach and later coached Seton Hall, while Alvin (Doggie) Julian was the second Boston coach and he later coached Dartmouth. Red Auerbach became head man on the Celtic bench in 1950-51 and served until 1964-65.
51. Maurice Podoloff, one of two brothers who owned the Arena in New Haven, Conn., became commissioner of the N.B.A. in 1946 when it was first formed as the Basketball Association of America and remained until September 1, 1963, when he was succeeded by Walter Kennedy. Lawrence O'Brien became the third N.B.A. commissioner in 1975.
52. Kennedy resigned as Mayor of Stamford, Conn. to accept the N.B.A. commissionership.

53. Jack and Lester Harrison owned the Rochester Royals. Forming the club in 1945, largely with returning veterans from World War II, they installed the team in the National Basketball League.
54. Oscar Robertson made 7,694 free throws out of 9,185 attempts in his career with the Cincinnati Royals for a percentage of .838.
55. Hal Greer who played for the Syracuse Nationals and then for the Philadelphia 76ers when the Nats shifted to Philadelphia in 1963.
56. The seven are: Hal Greer (3,855), Dolph Schayes (3,664), Walt Bellamy (3,536), Bailey Howell (3,498), Bill Bridges (3,375), Lenny Wilkens (3,285), and Tom Sanders (3,044).
57. Dolph Schayes played 16 seasons (in the N.B.A. from 1949-50 to 1963-64 and in the National League in 1948-49 when he was selected Rookie of the Year out of N.Y.U.), virtually all with the Syracuse Nationals. He moved to Philadelphia when the club became the 76ers in 1963 and later served as supervisor of officials for the N.B.A. and as a coach in the league. Ned Irish, president of the New York Knicks, once offered to buy the entire Syracuse franchise just to acquire Schayes for the Knicks.
58. The most obvious choice is Gene Conley who played parts of six seasons in the N.B.A. including two on championship Celtic teams and also had a major league baseball career which stretched from 1952 with the Boston Braves to 1963 with the Red Sox. Other possibilities include pitcher Dick Ricketts, shortstop Dick Groat, pitcher Cotton Nash, pitchers Dave DeBusschere, Steve Hamilton and Ron Reed. Extending a point, Frank Baumholtz and Kevin Connors might also count although they played pro basketball before the N.B.A. assumed its present form in 1949.
59. Wes Unseld. He paired twice with Gus Johnson and twice with Elvin Hayes as tandem 1,000-rebounders. Baltimore did it in 1963-64 with Johnson and Walt Bellamy. Detroit achieved the oddity first in 1960-61 with Bailey Howell and Walter Dukes. Other teams which have done it include the Knicks once, Celtics once, Warriors three times, and Hawks and Lakers once each.
60. Sid Borgia, who was famous for his bald pate, shrill voice and numerous arguments with Wilt Chamberlain who is about 20 inches taller.
61. Wilt Chamberlain in 1960-61 with the Philadelphia Warriors.
62. Nate (Tiny) Archibald had 910 for the K.C.-Omaha Kings in 1972-73.
63. Chamberlain in 1960-61 when he scored 2,707 points. Jack Twyman of Cincinnati was second in scoring with 2,338 points, the closest any veteran in the league came to the rookie.
64. The all-time all-star is Bob Cousy. After a standout career at Holy Cross, Cousy was bypassed in the draft by the Boston Celtics and was chosen by the Tri-Cities Blackhawks. Since Tri-Cities didn't really want him either, they traded him to the staggering Chicago Stags for a veteran player. Then Chicago folded prior to the start of the season and a lottery was held for two of their stars and rookie Cousy, the lone remaining man on the Stag roster. The Warriors and Knicks won the lottery for the first two choices and Boston was stuck with Cousy. He played 14 years, becoming one of the biggest names in pro basketball history, averaging 18.4 points per game, recording a then-record 6,955 assists and virtually rewriting the book on backcourt play for the pro game.

ANSWERS / NATIONAL BASKETBALL ASSOCIATION / 33

65. Alex Hannum coached the 1958 St. Louis Hawks and the 1967 Philadelphia 76ers, the only two teams to win N.B.A. titles other than the Boston Celtics from 1956-57 to 1968-69.
66. The two unfortunate coaches were Roy Rubin, who left a successful career at Long Island U., and Kevin Loughery, later coach of the A.B.A. New York Nets. Rubin was 4-47 before being supplanted by Loughery who was 5-26 for the balance of the season.
67. Bill Russell. Wilt Chamberlain won it four times, Lew Alcindor (Kareem Abdul-Jabbar) three times, Bob Pettit twice, and Bob Cousy, Oscar Robertson, Wes Unseld, Willis Reed, Dave Cowens and Bob McAdoo once each.
68. There are none. No guard has ever led the N.B.A. in floor-shooting accuracy, all winners being either centers or forwards.
69. Chuck Cooper of Duquesne was the first black signed by an N.B.A. club, although he didn't actually play in league games any sooner than Nat (Sweetwater) Clifton, the ex-Globetrotter who joined the Knicks. Both began play in 1949-50.
70. Sol Levy. His name was mentioned in testimony before a Grand Jury investigating the 1951 college basketball scandals during hearings conducted in 1952 and 1953. Commissioner Maurice Podoloff immediately dismissed Levy and no evidence of similar acts by an official of the N.B.A. has ever been uncovered.
71. Dan Biasone of the Syracuse Nationals. He introduced the suggestion at a clubowner's meeting in 1954. The time was arrived at on the basis of a study which indicated that N.B.A. teams took a shot every 18 seconds anyhow, and the rule was adopted to break up the "freeze and foul" techniques which were making a mockery of the sport.
72. Oscar Robertson ranks second in all-time career scoring behind Wilt Chamberlain with 26,710 points, and Elgin Baylor is fourth with 23,149 points. Neither ever won a scoring championship.
73. The three owner-coaches in 1954-55 were Clair Bee of the Baltimore Bullets, Les Harrison of the Rochester Royals and Eddie Gottlieb of the Philadelphia Warriors. The original Bullets franchise folded shortly after the start of that season and both Harrison and Gottlieb retired from coaching at the end of that season. The N.B.A. has not had a regular owner-coach since that season.
74. Neil Johnston of the Warriors in 1952-53. The Philadelphia center shot 45.2 from the floor and scored 1,564 points.
75. In Philadelphia, Paul Arixin (twice, 1951-52 and 1956-57), Neil Johnston (three times, 1952-53, 1953-54, (1954-55) and Wilt Chamberlain (three times, 1959-60, 1960-61, 1961-62) won scoring crowns for the Warriors. In San Francisco, Chamberlain (twice, 1962-63 and 1963-64) and Rick Barry (1966-67) turned the trick.

Bob Davies, super star of the Rochester Royals. Note: His uniform pants identify the Royals with the B. A. A.

Clyde Lovelette, Minneapolis Lakers, 1953.

Knick Vince Boryla grabs for ball along with Vern Mikkelson of Lakers.

Andy Phillip of the Chicago Stags, a charter member of the NBA, when it was called the Basketball Association of America.

38 / NATIONAL BASKETBALL ASSOCIATION

Paul Arizin and Jumping Joe Fulks, the first scoring champion of the NBA (then BAA).

Vern Mikkelson of Lakers takes shot against St. Louis. Hawks' Bob Petit watches along with Cliff Hagen of Minneapolis.

When Easy Ed Macauley played with Boston, he was part of the starry trio of Bob Cousy, Bill Sharman and Macauley. It was the Cooz to Easy to Charmin Sharman. Later he was traded to his hometown St. Louis Hawks.

Bob Petit was a super star with the St. Louis Hawks.

Dolph Schayes originally played with the NBL Syracuse Nationals, then became an NBA star when the two leagues merged.

Maurice Stokes of the Cincinnati Royals (left) was paralyzed with brain damage at the height of his career. A teammate, Jack Twyman, (above) established the Maurice Stokes fund. An annual benefit game is still played in the summer in his memory.

Knicks' Tom Gola

NATIONAL BASKETBALL ASSOCIATION / 45

1962 record setting Celtics, with coach Auerbach. Left to right; Bob Cousy, Tom Heinsohn, Sam Jones, and Jim Loscutoff.

Royals Oscar Robertson never won a title until he teamed up with Lew Alcindor at Milwaukee.

1964 Playoff action between San Francisco and Boston. Bill Russell tries to stop Wilt Chamberlain. Tom Heinsohn of Boston is Number 15.

A smiling Wilt the Stilt Chamberlain.

Bob Cousy

Elgin Baylor, the man with 1,000 moves. Baylor starred with the Minneapolis and Los Angeles Lakers.

Sam Jones when he was the Celtics top back court man.

The Boston Celtics John Havlicek, originally a super sub, later a super star.

Detroit's Terry Dischinger

Dave Bing

Jerry Lucas

Bill Bradley, star of two world champion New York Knickerbocker teams in 1970 and 1973.

NATIONAL BASKETBALL ASSOCIATION / 57

Bullets Wes Unseld stopping Willis Reed of the Knicks during 1969 Playoffs.

Rick Barry of the San Francisco Warriors.

Jerry West may have had the best outside touch of all time.

Earl Monroe started with the Baltimore Bullets. Later he teamed with Walt Frazier in the Knicks backcourt.

Bill Russell

Gail Goodrich

The Big "E" Elvin Hayes.

When the Knicks got Dave DeBusschere to work with Willis Reed and Bill Bradley up front they became champions.

Walt "Clyde" Frazier took Bob Cousy's place as the trickiest back court man.

"The Pistol" Pete Maravich, a big gunner with both the Atlanta Hawks and New Orleans Jazz.

Jerry West tries to maneuver around Phoenix' Connie Hawkins.

1972 Playoff action with Milwaukee's Kareem Abdul Jabbar going up against Lakers' Wilt Chamberlain.

Wes Unseld of the Bullets outrebounds Dave Cowens of the Celtics.

K. C. Jones, former star backcourt man with Boston, when he coached the Washington Bullets.

Lew Alcindor became Kareem Abdul Jabbar. He was a dominating factor, although different from either Bill Russell or Wilt Chamberlain.

Chapter 6

AMERICAN BASKETBALL ASSOCIATION / QUESTIONS

1. What season did the A.B.A. begin operation?
2. How many teams were there during the first A.B.A. season?
3. There are three charter members of the A.B.A. which operated in 1975-76 in the same cities they did during the league's first year. Name the teams.
4. The New York began their A.B.A. during the 1972 expansion?
5. What club came into the A.B.A. during the 1972 expansion?
6. During the first A.B.A. season two teams won over 50 games each but neither operated in the same city the following season. Name these two clubs and the cities they moved to after the inaugural A.B.A. season.
7. Who were the two finalists in the first A.B.A. championship playoff series and who won?
8. Two charter members of the A.B.A. folded after the 1971-72 season. Name them.
9. The team now known as the St. Louis Spirits previously operated in two other areas under other names. What was the club called in its prior locations?
10. Who was the first scoring champion of the A.B.A.?
11. What man set a record for most points in a season and failed to lead the A.B.A. in scoring?
12. When and where was the smallest playoff attendance in A.B.A. history?
13. Name the commissioners of the A.B.A.
14. One club in A.B.A. history moved from a city for one year and then moved back to the city from which it came for three more years. What was the city?
15. A charter franchise of the A.B.A. has operated in two different cities in the same state. Name the two cities.
16. What was the nickname of the Anaheim franchise in the A.B.A.?
17. The Utah franchise which disbanded early in the 1975-76 season had come to Salt Lake City from what other city in 1970?
18. Three teams have won the A.B.A. title and are no longer operating. Name them and the years they won the championships.
19. Two men have led the A.B.A. in scoring who also were the scoring champions of other pro leagues. name them and the other leagues which they led.
20. One man has won two A.B.A. scoring titles in successive seasons for two different teams. Name him and the teams he played for when he won the scoring titles.
21. A charter member of the A.B.A. has won a championship and shifted its franchise twice up to the 1975-76 season. What has the team been called in its three different locales?
22. What A.B.A. team drew the largest crowd in its history for the final game it ever played in the city it left?
23. Two so-called "regional" franchises in A.B.A. history regularly played their games in three different arenas in three different cities. Name the teams and the cities each called home.
24. In its first eight seasons, one team was a playoff finalist five times. Name the team.
25. What team has won the most A.B.A. championships? How many?

26. The A.B.A. record for most victories on the road in a single season has been achieved three times by different teams: Oakland, Indiana and Kentucky. How many games did they win away from their home floor?
27. Who holds the record for the most points by an individual in an A.B.A. season?
28. The record for victories in an A.B.A. season by a team is 68, set by a club which eventually lost in the championship playoff finals. What was the club and what year did they set the record?
29. By a quirk of scheduling, one man once played 90 games in the A.B.A. in a single season with an 84-game schedule. Who did it and how was it done?
30. A team once went through an A.B.A. schedule of 84 games and scored over 100 points only 31 times. Name the team and the year this happened.
31. Name the A.B.A. club once owned by a man who simultaneously owned a major league baseball club and a National Hockey League team.
32. Who holds the A.B.A. record for most rebounds in a season?
33. During the course of their first eight years, the New York Nets have played regular-season and playoff games in six arenas in the New York area. Name them.
34. What is the record for the most points by a team in a game and what team set the record?
35. Who is generally credited with the introduction of the red, white and blue basketball into the A.B.A.?
36. The most points ever scored by two teams in regulation time in the A.B.A. is 315. Name the two teams.
37. In its five seasons in Memphis, the franchise had three different nicknames. What were they?
38. Who holds the record for the most points by a player in an A.B.A. game?
39. What is the lowest number of franchises ever to finish an A.B.A. season?
40. What happened to the New Orleans franchise which was a charter member of the A.B.A.?
41. The record regular-season attendance in the A.B.A. is 16,621 for a single game. When did it happen and what teams played in the game?
42. Name the three teams that have won the 7-game championship final playoff series in A.B.A. history and the years in which they won them.
43. A team no longer in the A.B.A. set the league record for consecutive victories en route to a championship. Name the team and the number of games they won in a row.
44. What is the A.B.A. record for the least number of points scored by a team in a single quarter?
45. Four times in its first eight years the A.B.A. had a man selected as a Rookie of the Year who also made the first-team all-star squad selected at the end of the season. Name the four men who have achieved this distinction.
46. When and where was the first A.B.A. game ever played?
47. Three times in its history, the A.B.A. has had a team win the championship playoffs without placing a single man on the post-season all-league team. What were the three teams and the years they won the championship?
48. Over the years, ten cities have had both A.B.A. and N.B.A. teams either simultaneously or at different times. Name the ten cities.
49. Who is the all-time career scoring leader in A.B.A. history through 1974-75?
50. When and where was the first A.B.A. All-Star Game played?

ANSWERS / AMERICAN BASKETBALL ASSOCIATION

1. The American Basketball Association was formalized on February 2, 1967, and operated its first season in 1967-68.
2. There were 11 franchises in the A.B.A. during the 1967-68 season.
3. The three charter members who survived the first nine seasons in the same cities are Denver, Indiana (Indianapolis), and Kentucy (Louisville).
4. The New York Nets were originally the New Jersey Americans in 1967-68 and played their home games in the Teaneck (N.J.) Armory. They shifted to New York in the summer of 1968.
5. The San Diego team then called the Conquistadors, later known as the Sails. The team folded in 1975.
6. Pittsburgh with a record of 54-24 and Minnesota with 50-28 finished one-two in the Eastern Division in 1967-68. The Pipers moved to Minnesota the next season after the Muskies had gone to Miami.
7. The two finalists in the first A.B.A. playoff finals ever in 1968 were the Pittsburgh Pipers and the New Orleans Buccaneers. Pittsburgh won the series, 4 games to 3, and the championship.
8. The two charter members (1967-68) of the A.B.A. who went out of business after the 1971-72 season were the Miami Floridians and Pittsburgh. Miami began as the Minnesota Muskies and moved to Miami in 1968.
9. The Spirits were originally the Houston Mavericks from 1967-68 to 1969, when they moved to Carolina and became the Cougars. In 1974-75 they shifted to St. Louis.
10. Connie Hawkins of the Pittsburgh Pipers scored 1,875 points in 1967-68 to become the first scoring champion of the A.B.A.
11. Larry Jones of Denver scored 2,133 points in 1968-69, a league record at the time for most points in a season, but did not lead the A.B.A. in scoring because Rick Barry with 1,190 points in 35 games had a higher average per game (34.0).
12. The smallest playoff attendance in A.B.A. history was in the Western finals in 1969-70 when Dallas beat Los Angeles, 116-104, at the Los Angeles Sports Arena on April 20, 1970. The attendance was 971.
13. From 1967 to 1976 there were six commissioners of the A.B.A. plus another who acted on an interim basis. The six were: George Mikan, Jack Dolph, Robert Carlson, Mike Storen, Tedd Munchak and Dave DeBusschere. Jim Garden, president of the Carolina Cougars, was an interim commissioner between Dolph and Carlson.
14. Pittsburgh was the city. When the Pipers won the A.B.A. title in 1967-68 but didn't draw well, they moved to Minnesota where the territory had been vacated by a previous club (the Muskies). After one unsuccessful season in Minnesota, the Pipers moved back to Pittsburgh where they languished for three more seasons before expiring at the end of the 1971-72 campaign.
15. Dallas and San Antonio both served as home base for a team known initially as the Dallas Chapparals and later the San Antonio Spurs.
16. The Anaheim team of 1967-68 was called the Amigos.
17. The Utah Stars were originally the Los Angeles Stars and they moved to Salt Lake City when competition with the established L.A. Lakers proved too tough. The team started in Anaheim in 1967-68, played two years in L.A. (1968-70) and then went to Utah.

18. The three championship teams no longer operating are Pittsburgh, Oakland and Utah. Pittsburgh won in 1967-68, the Oaks in 1968-69 and Utah in 1970-71.
19. Rick Barry and Connie Hawkins. Barry was the N.B.A. champ in 1966-67 at San Francisco and led the A.B.A. in 1968-69 at Oakland, while Hawkins led the American Basketball League in 1961-62 with the Pittsburgh Rens and topped the A.B.A. in 1967-68 with the Pittsburgh Pipers.
20. Julius Erving led the A.B.A. in scoring in 1972-73 for the Virginia Squires and in 1973-74 for the New York Nets, having been traded by Virginia to New York in the off-season.
21. The team was originally called the Oakland Oaks (it won the title in 1968-69), then moved to Washington as the Capitals for the 1969-70 season and, in 1970, became the Virginia Squires.
22. The Los Angeles Stars attracted 8,233 for their final game. It was the last game of the league championship playoff series on May 25, 1970, when the Stars were beaten by Indiana, 111-107, at the L.A. Sports Arena. The game was, of course, the last one of the A.B.A. season and the following year the Stars were in Utah.
23. The Carolina Cougars played in Charlotte, Greensboro, and Raleigh, N.C. from 1969-70 to 1973-74, and the Virginia Squires play in Hampton, Richmond and Norfolk, Va.
24. The Indiana Pacers were finalists in 1969, 1970, 1972, 1973, and 1975.
25. The Indiana Pacers won the championship playoffs in 1970, 1972 and 1973, giving them three titles, more than any other club. No other team won more than once in the first eight seasons of the league.
26. The record is 28 achieved by Oakland in 1968-69, Indiana in 1970-71 and Kentucky in 1971-72.
27. The single-season record for total points is 2,538 set by Dan Issel of the Kentucky Colonels in 1971-72.
28. Kentucky in 1971-72 won 68 games and lost the playoff finals to Utah, 4 games to 3.
29. Chuck Williams played 90 games in 1973-74 by virtue of being traded in mid-season from a club which had played more games than most of the other clubs to one which had played the most at that point in the schedule. Williams played 57 games with San Diego and 33 with Kentucky.
30. In 1973-74 the San Antonio Spurs scored over 100 points in only 31 games.
31. The Memphis franchise was owned by Charles O. (for Owner) Finley when he also owned the Oakland A's baseball team and the Oakland Seals of the N.H.L. The Memphis club was then called the Tams because of Memphis' position on the Mississippi River at the conjunction of Tennessee (T), Arkansas (A) and Missouri (M).
32. Spencer Haywood of Denver with 1,637 in 1969-70.
33. The Nets have played in the Teaneck Armory (as the New Jersey Americans), the Long Island Arena in Commack, the Island Garden in West Hempstead, the Nassau Coliseum in Uniondale, Madison Square Garden, and the Felt Forum, a 5,000-seat arena which is part of the Madison Square Garden Center complex. Of course, the Nassau Coliseum has been thrie regular home since it opened in 1971.
34. The Indiana Pacers scored 177 points against the Pittsburgh Pipers at Indianapolis on April 12, 1970.

ANSWERS / AMERICAN BASKETBALL ASSOCIATION / 77

35. George Mikan, former all-time all-pro star and first commissioner of the A.B.A.
36. Miami defeated Dallas, 160-155, at Miami on March 22, 1970.
37. The club was known initially as the Memphis Pros, then as the Tams during the Finley era and, finally, as the Memphis Sounds.
38. The record is 67 points scored by Larry Miller of the Carolina Cougars against Memphis on March 8, 1972, at Greensboro, N.C.
39. Seven, the total which finished out the 1975-76 season. The season was expected to begin with ten clubs, but the Baltimore Crabbers folded before the season started and both the San Diego Sails and Utah Stars collapsed during the season.
40. After three seasons in New Orleans, the Buccaneer franchise was shifted to Memphis.
41. It was November 13, 1972, at Freedom Hall in Louisville when the Indiana Pacers meet the Kentucky Colonels that the record attendance of 16,621 for a regular-season A.B.A. game was established.
42. The three 7-game championship final playoff series are Pittsburgh over New Orleans in 1967-68, Utah over Kentucky in 1970-71 and Indiana over Kentucky in 1972-73. No team has ever swept the playoff finals.
43. The A.B.A. record for consecutive victories by a team is 16 set by the Oakland Oaks from December 10, 1968, to January 19, 1969.
44. Believe it or not, the least points scored by an A.B.A. team in a full quarter is 8. The four times this has happened were Nov. 9, 1967, when the Minnesota Muskies were held to 8 by Kentucky at Louisville; March 19, 1970, Denver at Pittsburgh; March 30, 1970, Carolina at Kentucky, and Dec. 12, 1973, San Antonio vs. Kentucky at San Antonio. San Antonio is the only club held to the record low on its own floor and the first three times it occurred, the 8-point period was the fourth quarter.
45. The four men who have been Rookie of the Year and a member of the post-season all-star squad in the same season in the A.B.A. are Mel Daniles, Indiana (1968), Spencer Haywood, Denver (1970), Charlie Scott, Virginia (1971) and Artis Gilmore, Kentucky (1972).
46. The A.B.A. opened its inaugural season on Friday, October 13, 1967, at the Oakland Coliseum with the Oakland Oaks defeating the Anaheim Amigos, 134-129. Oakland's Willie Porter scored the first basket in league history with 1:04 elapsed.
47. Utah in 1970-71, Indiana in both 1972-73 and 1971-72 are the three teams which have won the A.B.A. championship playoffs and failed to place a single man on the post-season all-star team.
48. The ten cities which have both N.B.A. and A.B.A. teams either at the same time or at different periods are New York, Indianapolis, Houston, St. Louis, Los Angeles, Washington, Oakland, New Orleans, Pittsburgh and San Diego. New York and Los Angeles have had them both at the same time.
49. Lou Dampier of Kentucky is the all-time career scoring leader of the A.B.A. with 12,658 points in eight seasons through 1974-75.
50. Indianapolis, January 9, 1968. The East won, 126-120.

Alex Hannum, a former coach with Syracuse in the NBA was the President-General Manager and Coach of the Denver Rockets for a time. Before that he coached the Oakland Oaks who had Rick Barry, the ABA's first real star.

Rick Barry made the New York Nets when he played with the team from Long Island for two seasons.

Spencer Haywood's presence with the Denver Rockets made ABA fans feel their product was the equal of the NBA. Alas, Haywood lasted only a short time.

The 1968-69
All League ABA team:

(top, left)
Connie Hawkins, Forward/Minnesota

(top, right)
Rick Barry, Forward/Oakland

(left)
Mel Daniels, Center/Indiana

(bottom, left)
Larry Jones, Guard/Denver

(below)
James Jones, Guard/New Orleans

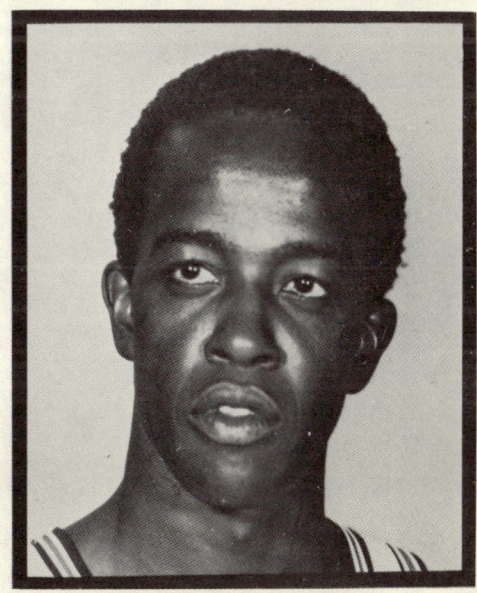

George McGinnis (30) with the Indiana Pacers against Carolina's Billy Cunningham.

The last ABA Commissioner Dave DeBusschere was formerly general manager of the New York Nets.

Mike Storen was the fourth commissioner of the ABA and also served as general manager of Kentucky and Memphis.

George Mikan, the former NBA hero, was the first commissioner of the ABA.

Wilt the Stilt Chamberlain spent one unhappy season coaching the San Diego Conquistidors.

That's George McGinnis of Indiana outrebounding the Nets Rick Barry and Billy Paultz in 1972.

Some rate New York's Julius Erving, shown trying to stop Jumping Joe Caldwell of Carolina, as the best player of all time.

Artis Gilmore was the best big man developed by the ABA.

Dan Issel, who played with Kentucky and Denver could be likened to an ABA Dave DeBusschere.

Lou Dampier was the all time champion of the home run, the 3 point ABA Bomb.

Chapter 7

TEAM AND LEAGUE NATIONAL BASKETBALL ASSOCIATION / QUESTIONS

1. The present structure of the N.B.A. was formed on June 6, 1946. What was the league known as at that time?
2. The new league faced competition from an older league established in 1937. Name the older league.
3. Four powerful teams jumped from the older league into the new organization for the 1948-49 season. Name the three teams.
4. In 1949, the two leagues merged into what is now known as the National Basketball Association. How many teams were there in the merged league?
5. How were the teams in the newly-merged league divided up for the 1949-50 season?
6. There are presently three teams in the N.B.A. which have a lineage older than the N.B.A. Name them.
7. There are three charter members of the N.B.A. from the 1946-47 season still operating franchises, though one is not in its original city. Name them.
8. In their early years, the New York Knicks played very few games in Madison Square Garden, although the club was owned by the big arena. Where did they play the bulk of their schedule?
9. The Boston Celtics, likewise, split their schedule between two buildings. Name their two home courts.
10. The Philadelphia Warriors played most of their games in Convention Hall. What other home court did they use extensively?
11. In 1951 a new rule was introduced which was designed to cut down the advantage of the strategic foul in the N.B.A. What did that rule call for?
12. What year was the 24-second rule introduced into the N.B.A.?
13. What was the first member of a major pro basketball league to be located outside of the United States?
14. Three different N.B.A. clubs have operated in Chicago. Name them.
15. Name the famous old semipro league which produced two teams that won B.A.A. championships.
16. Name the two teams which came out of this league to win the championships of the B.A.A.
17. What was the last N.B.A. team to go out of business during a season?
18. The Washington Bullets franchise has had five different team names during its history. What were those names?
19. What year did the Milwaukee Bucks come into the N.B.A.?
20. There are five cities which had charter franchises during the 1946-47 B.A.A. season, lost them, and now have other teams operating N.B.A. clubs in them. Name the five cities.
21. Only one expansion team has ever won the N.B.A. championship. What is that team?

22. Five cities have had teams which won N.B.A. titles and are now no longer presented in the league. Name the five cities.
23. When was the lowest scoring game in the N.B.A.'s history played and what was the score?
24. In 1975 the Warriors roared through the Washington Bullets in four straight games in the N.B.A. championship finals. Only twice before in league history had that happened. What were the other two 4-0 sweeps in the finals and what teams were involved?
25. Three times in N.B.A. history a team has won the championship playoff finals one year only to be beaten in the finals the following year. What teams have done this and when?
26. How many championship playoffs have the Boston Celtics won?
27. Two teams have gone to the finals three straight years and failed to win a championship. Name the teams and the years they acheived this dubious distinction.
28. In 1956-57 three teams tied for first place in the Western Division of the N.B.A. and they all had losing records. What were the three clubs?
29. What is the most points ever scored by a team in an N.B.A. game and what team did it?
30. What is the most points ever scored in the regulation game by a losing team in the N.B.A. and what team holds this record?
31. The Atlanta Hawks were based in three other cities during their N.B.A. history. Name the cities.
32. The record for most games won in a single season by a team is 69. Who accomplished this and what season did they do it?
33. What is the record for the largest margin of victory in an N.B.A. game and what teams were involved?
34. The Philadelphia 76ers franchise was originally a very famous club based in another city. What was the team formerly known as and where was it based?
35. Why were quarters in pro basketball originally set for 12 minutes each?
36. Three times N.B.A. clubs have started a season with 15 straight defeats. Name the three teams and the years in which this unfortunate occurrence befell them.
37. Name the three clubs which joined the N.B.A. in the 1970 expansion.
38. The Kansas City-Omaha Kings were based in two other cities before coming to their present location. What were those two cities and what was the club called then?
39. How many neutral-court games were played by N.B.A. clubs in the 1974-75 season?
40. A team once went through a schedule scoring 100 or more points in all but one of its games. How many 100-point games did this team have, what was the team and what year did it accomplish this record?
41. An N.B.A. club once had six men on its roster score 1,000 or more points in the same season. Name the team and the year this happened.
42. What is the record for the most defeats by an N.B.A. club in a single season and what team did it?
43. Two teams once combined for 160 free throw attempts in a five-overtime N.B.A. game. What two teams were involved?

44. An N.B.A. club once scored 100 or more points in 77 straight games. What club did this and what season did it happen?
45. What year did the Lakers move from Minneapolis to Los Angeles?
46. What team has played in the most N.B.A. finals?
47. In the history of the N.B.A., what team regularly played its games in the smallest-capacity building?
48. How many overtime periods were involved in the longest game in N.B.A. history?
49. The N.B.A. record for most average points per game by a team in a season is 125.4. What team set this record and what season was the record set?
50. One team has produced seven winners of the Podoloff Cup as the N.B.A.'s Most Valuable Player since the award was initiated in 1956. Name the team.

ANSWERS / TEAM AND LEAGUE
NATIONAL BASKETBALL ASSOCIATION

1. The organization was originally known as the Basketball Association of America.
2. The National Basketball League was organized in 1937.
3. The four clubs that jumped from the N.B.L. to the B.A.A. were the Minneapolis Lakers (with George Mikan), the Rochester Royals, the Ft. Wayne Pistons and the Indianapolis Jets.
4. There were 17 teams in the merged league which produced the National Basketball Association.
5. The 17 clubs were divided up into three divisions: the East and West of six teams each and the Central Division of five clubs. The East included Syracuse, New York, Boston, Washington, Philadelphia and Baltimore, the West consisted of Indianapolis, Anderson, Tri-Cities, Denver, Sheboygan and Waterloo. The Central was composed of Minneapolis, Rochester, Ft. Wayne, Chicago and St. Louis.
6. The three are the former N.B.L. clubs: Ft. Wayne, Minneapolis and Rochester which are still operating.
7. The three charter B.A.A. clubs still functioning are New York, Boston and the Golden State Warriors, previously based in Philadelphia and then San Francisco before moving to Oakland as Golden State.
8. The Knicks played most of their games at the 69th Regiment Armory, a 6,500-seat building located at 23rd St. and Lexington Ave., which they used until 1960 for some of their schedule. In 1946-47, the Knicks played only eight games in Madison Square Garden and 24 in the Armory. In later years, the number of games in the Armory steadily diminished.
9. The Celtics for many years played their games in both the Boston Garden, now their permanent home, and the smaller Boston Arena (capacity 5,000).
10. The Warrior games not played at Convention Hall due to conflict with other events were played at the old Philadelphia Arena where the team originated.
11. The new rule called for a jump ball after every foul so that the team commiting a deliberate strategic foul would not automatically gain possession of the ball after a free throw. It was clearly a failure since the teams with the height edge continued to commit fouls to gain control of the ball.
12. The 24-second rule was introduced in 1954 for the 1954-55 season.
13. The Toronto Huskies were members of the B.A.A. in its first season (1946-47) but lasted only one year.
14. The original Chicago N.B.A. team was a B.A.A. club called the Chicago Stags which operated from 1946-47 until 1949-50. The second was an expansion club of 1960 which lasted two years (1960-61 as the Packers and 1961-62 as the Zephyrs). The third is the present Chicago Bulls club which entered the N.B.A. in 1966 as an expansion team.
15. The American Basketball League operated largely on the Eastern seaboard for decades and was dominated by the Original Celtics in the mid-1920's.
16. The Philadelphia Warriors were developed from the Sphas (South Philadelphia Hebrew Association) club of the American League, and the Baltimore Bullets stepped out of the American League into the N.B.A. to win the title in 1947-48.
17. The Baltimore Bullets, original club folded on November 27, 1954.

ANSWERS / TEAM AND LEAGUE N.B.A. / 97

18. The present Washington Bullet club was known as the Chicago Packers and Zephyrs for two years in Chicago, moved to Baltimore in 1963, became the Capital Bullets in 1973 playing many games at the University of Maryland's Cole Fieldhouse in College Park, Md. prior to the opening of the new Capital Centre in Landover, Md., and were renamed Washington in 1975.
20. The five cities which were members of the B.A.A. in 1946-47, which lost their original clubs and now have other teams are: Chicago, Cleveland, Detroit, Washington and Philadelphia.
21. The Milwaukee Bucks entered the N.B.A. in the 1968 expansion and won the championship in 1971 by defeating the Baltimore Bullets in the finals.
22. The five cities no longer in the N.B.A. which have had championship teams are Baltimore (1948), Minneapolis (five times, 1949, 1950, 1952, 1953, 1954), Rochester (1951), Syracuse (1955), and St. Louis (1958).
23. The lowest scoring game was a 19-18 victory by Ft. Wayne over Lakers at Minneapolis on November 22, 1950. The Pistons held the ball against the powerful Lakers and succeeded in winning on the road against the league's best club, but the game itself was a travesty. Ft. Wayne scored 8 points in the first quarter and it was the highest-scoring quarter of the game. The Lakers got one point in the fourth period, the Pistons three. Each team made four baskets, Ft. Wayne having an 11-10 edge in free throws to win. George Mikan scored 15 points, the only man in double figures and got all four of the Lakers' baskets. Ft. Wayne had only 13 field goal attempts, Minneapolis 18.
24. The other two 4-0 sweeps in the finals were in 1959 when Boston beat Minneapolis and 1971 when Milwaukee defeated Baltimore. Boston wrapped up its sweep in five days from April 4 to 9, by scores of 118-115, 128-108, 123-120 and 118-113. Milwaukee won on April 21, 1971, 98-88, followed with 102-83 and 107-99 victories before closing out the series, 118-106, at Baltimore on April 30.
25. The Philadelphia Warriors won the finals in 1947 and lost to Baltimore in 1948, the Boston Celtics won in 1957 and lost to St. Louis in 1958 and the Los Angeles Lakers won in 1972 and were beaten by the New York Knicks in 1973.
26. The Celtics have been in the finals 13 times and have won 12 championships, losing only to St. Louis in 1958.
27. The Knicks were beaten in the finals in 1951 by Rochestr, and in 1952 and 1953 by Minneapolis, while the L.A. Lakers lost to Boston in 1968 and 1969 and to New York in 1970.
28. St. Louis, Ft. Wayne and Minneapolis were all 34-38 in the Western Division in 1956-57. St. Louis won playoff games against the Pistons and Lakers for the first playoff spot. The fourth (and last)-place Rochester Royals were 31-41. St. Louis ultimately played its way to the finals only to lose to Boston, giving the Celtics their first title.
29. The Boston Celtics scored 173 against the Minneapolis Lakers on February 27, 1959, at the Boston Garden.
30. The record is the 151 scored by the San Diego Rockets in a losing effort at the Cincinnati Gardens against the Royals on March 12, 1970.
31. The Atlanta Hawks began their N.B.A. career in 1949-50 as the Tri-Cities Blackhawks based in Moline, Ill., after joining in the merger from the National Basketball League into the N.B.A. They moved to Milwaukee in 1951, St. Louis in 1955 and Atlanta in 1968.

32. The Los Angeles Lakers won 69 games in an 82-game schedule (a percentage of .841) in 1971-72 and that team won the only N.B.A. title ever in Los Angeles.
33. The record is 63 posted by Los Angeles over San Francisco, 162-99, on March 19, 1972.
34. Formed in 1946-47, the current 76ers were originally the Syracuse Nationals of the National Basketball League. The club joined the N.B.A. in the 1949 merger and after playing in three finals and winning a championship in 1955, the club was shifted to Philadelphia in 1963.
35. At the time the B.A.A. was founded in 1946, collegiate games were played in four 10-minute quarters. The pro game was made 12 minutes so that one game would provide a full evening's activity without necessitating a doubleheader. Of course, the N.B.A. for many years played twinbills anyhow to fill its bigger buildings while the colleges went away from the practice after the 1951 scandal virtually ended the arena doubleheaders.
36. The three teams which started seasons with 15 straight losses were the Denver Nuggets in 1949-50, the Cleveland Cavaliers in 1970-71 and the Philadelphia 76ers in 1972-73.
37. The 1970 expansion clubs were Buffalo, Cleveland and Portland.
38. The Kansan City-Omaha Kings were originally the famous Rochester Royals, started by Les and Jack Harrison in 1945 in the National Basketball League. They joined the N.B.A. in 1948, moved to Cincinnati in 1957 and to Kansas City-Omaha in 1972.
39. Neutral-court games, usually as part of doubleheaders in other league cities or single games at major towns near one of the team's home courts, started in 1948-49. A total of 1,471 neutral-court games have been played in the N.B.A., but none in 1974-75. The single-season high was 90 in 1954-55.
40. In 1971-72 the Los Angeles Lakers scored 100 or more points in 81 out of the 82 games on their regular-season schedule.
41. The Syracuse Nationals in 1960-61 had six men score over 1,000 points. The six were Dolph Schayes (1,868), Hal Greer (1,551), Dick Barnett (1,320), Dave Gambee (1,085), Larry Costello (1,084) and Johnny Kerr (1,056).
42. The record for futility is 73 losses in a single season by the Philadelphia 76ers in 1972-73.
43. The two clubs were the Syracuse Nationals and the Anderson Packers at Syracuse on November 24, 1949. Syracuse had 86 charity shots and Anderson 74.
44. New York scored 100 or more in 77 successive games in 1966-67 but the Knicks finished fourth in the Eastern Division and were eliminated in the first round of the playoffs.
45. The Lakers moved to Los Angeles in 1960. The team originated in Chicago as the Chicago American Gears and moved to Minneapolis when the B.A.A. got the franchise to play in the Chicago Stadium in 1946-47. As the Minneapolis Lakers, the team built around George Mikan dominated the N.B.A. for six seasons, winning five titles from 1948-49 to 1953-54.
46. The Lakers have played in a record 15 N.B.A. finals, six while based in Minneapolis and nine in Los Angeles. But the club has won only one of the nine since moving to L.A. after having taken 5 out of 6 when calling Minneapolis home.

47. The Ft. Wayne Pistons joined the N.B.A. in 1948 and until the opening of Memorial Coliseum in 1952, the club played its home games in the North Side High School Gymnasium which seated 3,800.
48. Six. The Rochester Royals and Indianapolis Olympians on January 6, 1951, with Indianapolis finally winning, 75-73. The low score was produced when both teams elected to hold the ball after winning the opening tap-off at the start of each of the overtimes and playing for one shot with the Olympians finally making a basket in the sixth overtime.
49. The Philadelphia Warriors in 1961-62. The team finished second.
50. The Boston Celtics. The winners include Bob Cousy (once), Bill Russell (five times) and Dave Cowens (once).

Vince Boryla

TEAM AND LEAGUE N.B.A. / 101

Red Auerbach

The Referee's Dean, Mendy Rudolph.

Former NBA Commissioner Walter Kennedy.

Chapter 8

GENERAL INFORMATION / QUESTIONS

1. Name the man who coached an N.F.L. team in the Super Bowl and also played in the N.B.A.
2. Name three teams which won 60 or more games in two or more successive N.B.A. or A.B.A. seasons.
3. This man was one of the first full-time trainers in the N.B.A. and also was used as a fill-in coach for both the New York Knicks and the Detroit Pistons. Name him.
4. Nine N.B.A. All-Star Games have been played in cities which no longer hold N.B.A. franchises. Name five of these cities.
5. When and where was the first N.B.A. All-Star Game played?
6. Name the winning coach and the losing coach in the first N.B.A. All-Star Game.
7. Which N.B.A. team drafted Bill Russell?
8. Who was the first man selected as coach of the year in the A.B.A.?
9. What former A.B.A. coach later became a referee in the league?
10. Although two early-round games previously produced games where the winning team scored over 100 points, name the team which won a game in the championship final playoff round with over 100 points in a game for the first time and the year it occurred.
11. Name the man who appeared as a participant in the N.B.A. championship final series two straight seasons without being a player on any of the teams involved.
12. What was the real name of the late Goose Tatum, long-time star of the Harlem Globetrotters?
13. In the mid-1950's Goose Tatum, Marquis Haynes and others broke away from the Globetrotters and formed their own touring comedy basketball team. What was the team originally called?
14. A member of the N.B.A. Eastern division once played a Western Division schedule. Name the year and the team which was in this unusual position.
15. What member of the American Basketball Association had two different nicknames before its initial season of play and never played a league game?
16. What executive of the A.B.A. also served as an advisor to the American Football League before its merger with the N.F.L.?
17. In 1949-50 there were 17 teams in the merged National Basketball Association. Which one of them had the best regular season record?
18. What is the least number of playoff games a team has needed to win the A.B.A. championship?
19. Name the first five men selected to the initial N.B.A. All-Defensive team chosen after the 1968-69 season.
20. What club president during the A.B.A. inaugural season later served as the commissioner of pro leagues in two other sports?
21. The Milwaukee Bucks were the first N.B.A. expansion team in modern years to reach the final round of the playoffs (in 1970-71). Name the second such team.
22. Name the charter member teams in the first season of the Basketball Association of America in 1946-47.

23. Both the B.A.A. and the A.B.A. began their first seasons (1946-47 and 1967-68, respectively) with the same number of teams. What was the number?
24. Name four referees who worked in both the N.B.A. and A.B.A.
25. Name two important positions held by N.B.A. commissioner Larry O'Brien outside of the sports world before he became N.B.A. commissioner.
26. The New Jersey Americans drew only 43,195 fans during the 1967-68 A.B.A. season at the Teaneck Armory. But they compiled one of the best home records in the league. What was their record on the Armory court?
27. The Bridgeport (Conn.) team in the Eastern Pro Basketball League once included such stars as former Knick Ralph Kaplowitz. Now defunct, the team was sponsored by an oil company. Name the company.
28. In 1949-50, a team from the Pennsylvania coal mining regions won the Eastern Pro League championship. What was the team?
29. One of the most famous college all-Americans of the 1940's became famous for not playing pro ball. Name him.
30. Name the rookie of the year in the A.B.A. for the 1974-75 season?
31. Name the A.B.A. team which made the final round in alternating even-numbered years, twice winning the championship.
32. Name the A.B.A. team which moved into a city immediately after the close of a season in which an A.B.A. club folded in the city to which they moved.
33. Who was the pro basketball player who became a city councilman in the city in which he starred as a rookie for a championship N.B.A. team?
34. How many games did the New York Nets need in the final round to defeat the Denver Nuggets for the 1976 A.B.A. championship?
35. Name three arenas used by pro basketball teams playing in Indianapolis, Ind.

ANSWERS / GENERAL INFORMATION

1. Bud Grant, head coach of the Minnesota Vikings in the Super Bowl in 1970, 1974 and 1975, played for the Minneapolis Lakers in the N.B.A. in 1949-50 and 1950-51.
2. There are four choices: Denver (A.B.A.), 1975-76 and 1974-75, Milwaukee (N.B.A.) 1972-73, 1971-72 and 1970-71, Los Angeles (N.B.A.) 1972-73 and 1971-72, and Philadelphia (N.B.A.) 1967-68 and 1966-67.
3. Don Friedrichs
4. St. Louis hosted three, and six other cities had one each, including Cincinnati, Rochester, Syracuse, Baltimore, San Diego, and Fort Wayne.
5. The first N.B.A. All-Star Game was played at the Boston Garden on March 2, 1951.
6. The East, coached by the late Joe Lapchick, defeated the West, coached by Johnny Kundla, 111-94.
7. The St. Louis Hawks drafted Bill Russell and traded him to Boston while he was representing the U.S. in the 1956 Olympic Games at Melbourne, Australia.
8. Vine Cazetta of the Pittsburgh Pipers was coach of the year in 1968 in the A.B.A.
9. Joe Belmont coached the Denver Rockets (now Nuggets) and shared coach of the year honors in 1970 with Bill Sharman of the Los Angeles Stars before becoming an A.B.A. referee.
10. Minneapolis, on April 23, 1950, was the first team ever to score over 100 points in a game in the N.B.A. finals when the Lakers beat Syracuse, 110-95, at Minneapolis in the sixth game of their final series to win the title. Previous to that game only two games in any round of the playoffs produced 100-point scores (both by the N.Y. Knicks).
11. Charlie Eckman was the man. He refereed the finals between Minneapolis and Syracuse in 1954 and coached the Fort Wayne Pistons in the finals against Syracuse the following year.
12. Goose Tatum's real first name was Reese.
13. The breakaways formed a club known as the Harlem Magicians, later to become the Fabulous Magicians.
14. The Syracuse Nationals played a Western Division schedule in 1950-51 owing to the 17-team league created by the merger of the B.A.A. with the N.B.L. to form the N.B.A.
15. The Baltimore franchise, scheduled to begin play in 1975-76, was originally called the Hustlers, a name later changed to Crabbers. But the team folded before the season opened.
16. Thurlo McCrady, the executive director of the A.B.A., was originally a consultant to Commissioner Joe Foss when the American Football League began in 1960.
17. The Syracuse Nationals who finished with a 51-13 record overall, including an astonishing 34-1 at home in the State Fair Coliseum.
18. 14 games (12-2) by the New York Nets in 1973-74.
19. The first N.B.A. All-Defensive team included Walt Frazier and Dave DeBusschere of New York, Bill Russell of Boston, Nate Thurmond of San Francisco and Jerry Sloan of Chicago.
20. Gary Davidson was the president of the Dallas Chaparalls during the 1967-68 season and later served as commissioner of the World Hockey Association and the World Football League.

21. The second expansion team to reach the N.B.A. finals in modern times was the Phoenix Suns in 1975-76 when they faced the Boston Celtics. The Suns joined the N.B.A. in 1968-69, the same season as Milwaukee.
22. The charter members of the B.A.A. in 1946-47 were New York, Boston, Philadelphia, Providence, Toronto, Washington, Chicago, St. Louis, Cleveland, Pittsburgh and Detroit.
23. Both the B.A.A. and the A.B.A. began their first seasons with eleven teams.
24. The choices include Norm Drucker, Joe Gushue, John Vanak, Jack Madden and Ed Rush.
25. O'Brien was formerly chairman of the Democratic National Committee and also served as Postmaster General of the United States under President Johnson in 1965.
26. The Americans won 26 of their 40 games in the Teaneck Armory, but failed to make the playoffs due to their dismal 10-29 road record.
27. The Bridgeport Aerosols were sponsored by Standard Oil of Connecticut.
28. The Wilkes-Barre Barons.
29. Bob Kurland of Oklahoma A & M (now Oklahoma State) elected to join the semipro Phillips 66 Oilers of Bartlesville, Okla., one of the nation's leading A.A.U. teams rather than join either of the two major pro leagues of the day (the N.B.L. or the B.A.A.).
30. Marvin Barnes of the St. Louis Spirits was the 1975 Rookie of the Year in the A.B.A.
31. The New York Nets made the finals in 1972 and lost to Indiana in six games, then won the championship in 1974 and 1976.
32. St. Louis moved to Salt Lake City where the Utah Stars had gone bankrupt during the previous season, 1975-76.
33. Tom Gola, a college All-American at LaSalle College, was a star rookie with the Philadelphia Warriors when they won the 1956 N.B.A. title and later became a Philadelphia City Councilman.
34. The Nets defeated the Nuggets in six games, winning three at home in the Nassau Coliseum and one of three at McNichols Sports Arena in Denver.
35. The Indianapolis arena now being used is known as Market Square. The previous homes of pro basketball in Indianapolis included the 15,000-seat Butler University Fieldhouse and the smaller Fair Grounds Coliseum.

Chapter 9

GLOSSARY OF BASKETBALL SLANG

AIR BALL
A shot that completely misses both the basket and backboard.

BACK DOOR
A play in which one man cuts along the baseline toward the basket to take a pass from his teammate behind a screen from another teammate.

BACKCOURT
Either the two men who play guard on a team (known as backcourt men) or the area on the opposite side of the midcourt line from where the action is taking place.

BASELINE
The end lines of the court behind each basket across the opposite ends of the floor which define out-of-bounds.

BLOCK
A movement which illegally impedes the progress of a player on the other team.

BOARDS
The backboards, generally used when speaking in terms of rebounding ("this man really hits the boards").

BUCKET
The basket or scoring a goal ("he made three quick buckets").

BURN
To evade a defensive man assigned to you for a clear shot.

CAGERS
Describing players—derived from experimental games when the court was enclosed with mesh or wire to keep the ball in play continuously.

CHARITY SHOT
A free throw (a shot taken from the foul line or "the charity stripe").

CIRCLE
The area encircling the free throw line, generally considered a prime shooting zone.

CLUTCH
This one has several meanings, depending upon context, such as failing in the crucial moment (as in "choke up"), succeeding in the key moment (as in "he is a real clutch player") or the time of the game when the win or loss will be decided ("now it's a clutch situation").

D
Defense (a team tough on defense is said to play "good D").

DEADEYE
A consistently accurate shooter.

DEUCE
A basket scored (two points, "deuce" signifying two).

DUNK
Holding the ball above the basket and slamming it downward through the ring (sometimes called "a slam dunk," this move is not permitted in levels below professional).

FEEDER
A man who is known for his ability to set up his teammates for good shots.

GIVE AND GO
Handing or passing the ball off to a teammate and breaking quickly toward the basket for an easy shot by moving around the defensive man.

GIVE ONE
Particularly in the pros, the act of committing a foul for the purpose of getting the ball back on offense when your team has not exceeded the allowed number of fouls in a period to incur additional penalty shots, essentially trading (or "giving") one shot for one point for one shot for a possible two points when your team regains control after the free throw.

GUNNER
A player who shoots the ball almost every time he gets possession in the offensive zone (also known as "clucker," "heaver," etc.)

HATCHET MAN
A player who is notorious for his use of rough tactics, usually on the star players of the other team.

HOOP
The basket or the scoring of a goal ("give it to Sid for a quick hoop").

KEY
The former name of the free throw shooting circle and lane; before the lane was widened to 12 feet, the layout resembled a keyhole since the circle at the top was 12 feet wide and the lane between the circle and basket only 6 feet.

LANE
The path between the free throw circle and the basket, now 12 feet in width.

LAST TWO
Final two minutes of each period in a pro game in which special rules apply ("it's the first foul in the last two").

OSCAR JOB
A performance by a player which enabled him to draw a foul on his opponent from the officials when, in reality, there was little or no contact between the two, his acting work being of Academy Award level to fool the officials (hence earning him "an Oscar").

PICK AND ROLL
A play in which one man screens out an opponent for his teammate with the ball, then rolls off the screening position toward the basket to take a pass from that teammate.

REJECT
The act of a defensive man batting away or "rejecting" a shot by the opposition without committing a goal-tending infraction.

SCREEN
The act of positioning yourself so as to block the path of a defensive man on the other team who is guarding a teammate so that your man may get free for a shot.

SHOWBOAT
A player who employs elaborately fancy dribbles, passes and moves, sometimes for the purpose of humiliating the other team or the man guarding him.

SKIPPER
A nickname sometimes applied to coaches.

STUFF
Another term with a dual meaning, either literally stuffing the ball into the basket or having it "stuffed" by a defensive player who bats it away before it reaches the basket.

SWISH
A shot which goes cleanly through the basket with hitting the rim.

TIME LINE
The line dividing the court into two equal halves and used, among other reasons, for the application of the 10-second rule which requires a team to bring the ball out of the backcourt into the attacking zone within that period of time.

TWINE
The netting below the rim of the basket (also called "cords", "strings", "net", etc.)

ZONE
A defensive system in which the five players divide the court up into areas for coverage rather than attaching themselves to the five men on the other club (man-to-man); the zone is not legal in the pro leagues.